Published 2024 by New Haven Publishing
www.newhavenpublishingltd.com   newhavenpublishing@gmail.com

Cover design by Jeffrey Morgan and Pete Cunliffe. Interior design by Pete Cunliffe: pcunliffe@blueyonder.co.uk

" Ladies and gentlemen,

it pleases me very much this evening

to introduce to you a most *powerful* band,

The Stooges! "

English translation from the original German
text of the address to the troops made nightly
during the 1973-1974 *Raw Power* campaign
by Stoogestaffel Field Marshal Ron Asheton (ret.)

DEDICATION

✝

Jeffrey Morgan dedicates his life to Jesus Christ (John 3:16-17);
his life's work to the glory of God (1 Corinthians 10:31);
and he thanks the Holy Spirit for keeping him
on the narrow path (Matthew 7:13-14).

✝

This is a new phase **STOOGES** book . . .

essential to the content of the biography was that they spoke

live for many hours; in comes the warmth and the freshness

of a new edition; as reproduced for print by the authors.

IGGY AND THE STOOGES

The Authorized Biography

Archived, Assembled, and Written by Jeffrey Morgan
with Robert Matheu
and Dave DiMartino, Ivan Suvanjieff, Brian J. Bowe
plus James Williamson, Shepard Fairey

Photographed by Robert Matheu
with John Catto, Robert Sikora, Jeff Magnum
and Carlos Llano, Frankie N. Carranza
plus Jeffrey Morgan, Ralph Alfonso

Artwork by Shepard Fairey

Designed by Pete Cunliffe

This is an actual telling of The Stooges' story. It has been assembled to be read in sequence from the first page through to the last page without interruption. In order to present a true historical documentation of the band in person, editing of any nature has been avoided. The spoken content of all interviews has been left totally unchanged from the original tapes. There has been no technical assistance added to this biography, such as formatting, and all events are presented here exactly as they occurred.

Telling the story of The Stooges was a challenge of unprecedented scope and complexity requiring a level of endurance from both men and machine previously unheard of in biography writing. Technical flaws, resulting from equipment failure as well as human overload, are inevitable in a venture of this size. Just as inevitably, some of them occur in the material included in this book. Consider them like the scars in fine leather, proof of the origin and authenticity of the material in which they are found.

This authorized biography was compiled from writing and interviews done in cities throughout the United States and Canada. Aside from the proofreading necessary to assemble the manuscript into book form, this volume is an organic documentary and absolutely livid!

INTRODUCTION
by James Williamson

I first met Ron Asheton and Jim Osterberg when I was 16. During the spring of 1966, I was home for spring break from the Anderson School in upstate New York. It was kind of a boarding school for fuck ups who didn't quite fit elsewhere. I had recently been let out of the Pontiac Juvenile Home where I had been sent for the horrible offense of being "incorrigible" because I was truant from school since I wouldn't cut my hair and couldn't come back until I did.

Prior to all that, I had formed a band with a local guy named Scott Richardson. Well, at least it became a band once we had recruited the remainder of another band at the Michigan State Fair. In any event, our band became the Chosen Few. Needless to say, my tenure was short lived due to my stay in Juvie.

As the time went on, the Chosen Few's bass player moved on. Through various connections they were able to land a cool bass player named Ron Asheton with super long hair. He was so cool that he played with his back to the audience; to hear his amp better, he claimed.

Anyway, the Chosen Few had a gig at a Frat Party in Ann Arbor, Michigan one weekend while I was home and they invited me to tag along and check out the band with this new guy Ron Asheton on bass.

As it turned out, a local guy named Jim Osterberg was also hanging out with Ron there that night. I had known of Jim Osterberg as the ace drummer for the Prime Movers. I had brought my guitar along for some reason I can't recall (probably just because). Anyway, I played a couple of my original tunes for Ron and Jim, and Jim in particular quite liked them. From that night forward, I stayed in touch with both of them as often as I could since I lived in the Detroit suburbs and they were in Ann Arbor area which was a fair drive away.

I would hang out at Ron's mother's house sometimes and later would hang out at Toad Hall on Forest, their first communal house consisting of Jim Osterberg, Ron and Scott Asheton, and Dave Alexander where the band idea was initially realized. Then later at the Fun House on Packard where eventually I was even living for a brief time until a couple of the guys, Bill Cheatum and Zeke Zettner (who by then were playing rhythm guitar and bass respectively in the band), invited me to go in on a house together in Ann Arbor.

Over the years from Toad Hall days to the Fun House days I saw the band play several local venues and was impressed by their stage presence and growth as a band. At that point I never dreamed I'd be playing in The Stooges, but one thing led to another and I ended up there. And later, I helped form a variation called "Iggy And The Stooges."

In one way or another, all of my years with The Stooges were filled with incredible experiences. Our little gang was truly so insular that the outside day-to-day world had less impact on us than it would assume. We conjured up music that defied most analysis and easy labels. It wasn't in the lexicon of the day and it took a long, long time to be accepted.

We created great things. May this book inspire *you* to great things of your own—or unthinkable depths, whichever applies.

thestooges

ROCK
ACTION

THE AUTHORIZED ILLUSTRATED STORY OF IGGY & THE STOOGES

Robert Matheu and Jeffrey Morgan

ALL ABOARD FOR FUNTIME

One of the great things about reprinting an authorized biography that's already been published is that you can look back in amusement and read the consumer reviews to see how successful the first version was. How soon they regret.

"The writing irritated me. It was all over the place. I am not expecting Joyce or Hemingway prose (this is a Stooges book). I just wasn't feeling the story. Kind of a shame. This is a great coffee table book that really does not need to be read to be enjoyed," wrote one disgruntled consumer after coughing up a hefty chunk of change to buy a copy of the original 2009 edition.

"Disappointing. The images are great but the text is misleading and incomplete. I found it expensive for such a lack of information text," assessed another unsatisfied customer who also dug deep and purchased the pricey hardcover.

These are but two examples of the online ire evoked, both of which contain accurate quotations; you could look it up. Robert Matheu did, to which he always cheerfully replied: "Whatever you *say*, buddy. If your money's *good*, your money's *good!*"

It goes without saying, but I'll say it anyway. There were those who took our book too seriously for the express reason that we refused to take The Stooges as seriously as *they* did. That's because what we wrote was fortified and infused with an ironclad rock 'n' roll sensibility best suited to our subject; one which steadfastly refused to adopt a highfalutin highbrow hoity-toity gasbag pseudo-intellectualism straight outta Musicology 101, thus denying them the opportunity to read and wallow in something staid and stuffy that reflected and reinforced their own intolerant narrow-minded prejudices of what a rock 'n' roll biography should be.

But for every tight energy emitter, there were many a wise Stoogesayer who recognized the lively irreverent myth-making humor in what we were doing, and who gave us perceptive payola-like praise that ranged from "The story of the Psychedelic Stooges told with CREEM-like reportage" and "A brilliant overview of

The Stooges" to "Fun to read" and "A very well written book" to my own personal favorite, the long-winded but nevertheless accurate "I like how they quote from Hitchcock's extended trailer to *Psycho* when referring to Ron's infamous memorabilia collection that you do not see, which every Stooges fan knows about anyway so why bother mentioning it again when everyone else already has?"

Not see, geddit? You could look up *those* quotes as well, but don'tcha dare do it now or you'll miss the inside yarn of how this whole Stooges shebang came to be, both then and now. So put down that *Racing Form* and pay attention 'cause I'm the only one that'll tell ya the truth and I tell ya I'm the one who knows.

*** *** ***

It all began when Robert dropped by one day in the spring of 2005 to inform me that he had received an Air Mail letter from Rome sent by Rosario Ciccarelli, the publisher of *Fun House* which, at my suggestion, was additionally and accurately tagged on the front cover and masthead as being "Italy's Only Rock 'n' Roll Magazine." Given the name, it was only a matter of time before Rosario would get around to cranking out an issue on The Stooges and, since we had both written for the Summer 2005 edition of *Fun House* which had centered around our mutual pal Lester Bangs, would we care to contribute to this new Stooges number as well?

Care we did, which is why the Autumn 2005 issue contained several of Robert's classic Stooges photographs as well as my own "Strisciando Dalla Casa Dei Divertimenti" (originally titled "Crawlin' From The Fun House"). But it wasn't until we received our contributor copies in the mail and flipped through them in a booth at Musso & Frank that we both began to wonder if this foreign edition didn't portend an even greater opportunity for us to expand upon. Then we ordered another round and promptly forgot all about it.

*** *** ***

It wasn't until I came across that Stooges issue of *Fun House* a year later that I remembered our fanciful conversation at Musso & Frank. I also recalled how

Fun House

Italy's Only Rock 'n' Roll Magazine

Numero 8 - Autunno 2005 - € 5,00

Robert Matheu
The Shootin' Gallery

The Fuzztones
Il culto del fuzz

HP Lovecraft
Uno scrittore heavy metal

Italia Noise 2005
Le nuove frontiere del noise

Fantasy Filmfest
Terrore a Berlino

George Harrison
Il Dark Horse dei Beatles

I fratelli Marx
Dal Comico al Surreale

Malleus & Ufomammut
Binomio discograficartistico

Fun House Collection Vol. 4
Mike Watt

thestooges
deluxe

Le ristampe dei primi due storici album

Mamzoux, the last of the Elder Hoodoo Queens, once predicted that I was destined to write an authorized rock star biography every ten years, beginning with Alice Cooper's in 1999. 2019 put paid to that prophesy, but back in 2006 such sagacity made perfect sense to me.

So I called Robert on the chatterline to remind him of our great notion to go forth and make Stooge disciples of all the nations when he cut me short. "Rama Lama! That's why we work so well together," he enthused. "Rosario, right? I was just thinking the same thing! How about if we do an authorized bio and call it "ROCK ACTION: THE AUTHORIZED ILLUSTRATED STORY OF IGGY & THE STOOGES"? Scott will *love* that! Let's do a cover design, write up a book proposal, and take it from there!" Write we did, adopting a tone of respectful irreverence that not only best reflected our decades-long wiseacre tenure at CREEM but the slapstick vaudeville comedy ethos of a rock band named after The Three Stooges, as evidenced by this excerpt from the fifth page of our proposal:

"There will also be a full detailed accounting of The Stooges' legendary BBC radio shows plus all of their worldwide television performances ranging from *Top Of The Pops* and *The Old Grey Whistle Test* to *Shindig* and *Hullabaloo*. Well, actually, there'll be no mention of any of them, since none exist. But we *will* list all of their infamous 'aborted due to flying projectiles' tour dates as well as a skewed glance askance at some of their best bootleg recordings.

"We will also enlist a bevy of stenographers to carefully listen to each Stooges album through headphones and finally provide us, once and for all, with a complete set of transcribed lyrics to every single Stooges song extant—assuming, of course, that any of them are able to decipher Iggy's own patented brand of Stoogespeak."

We then thought it wise to conclude the proposal by mentioning our qualifications, just in case anyone should dare to ask that musical question: *Why us?*

"Robert Matheu began his photo career down on the streets of Detroit, where he found his way to the earliest of Stooges shows in 1969 at a number of now-demolished dives like the legendary Smack Junction Saloon. From there he followed The Stooges through such Motor City vomitoriums as the Silver Spike Palace and the Mainline Arena before witnessing the truly legendary 'loser take all' shows that closed out The Stooges' first stint as a group together.

"Since then, Matheu's photographic career has found him crossing paths with The Stooges to this very day, photographing them live at the Hammersmith Apollo for their album *The Weirdness*. He also contributed photographs to, and was a consultant on, the recent Elektra Records deluxe two disc reissues of *The Stooges* and *Fun House*, as well as the Iggy Pop career retrospective *A Million In Prizes* and the live box set *Where The Faces Shine*. He similarly provided photographs and liner notes to The Stooges' box set *Heavy Liquid*. He has worn out more copies of *Fun House* than he cares to remember.

"Jeffrey Morgan met and shook hands with Moe Howard, Larry Fine, and Curly Joe DeRita in August 1962 after The Three Stooges performed on stage at the *CNE Grandstand Matinee Fun-Fest*. He has worn out more copies of *Raw Power* than he cares to remember."

Laugh if you will, but those breathless paragraphs of purple prose resulted in Abrams publishing *The Stooges: The Authorized And Illustrated Story* on October 1st, 2009.

*** *** ***

Beginning in 2017, we began to discuss reprinting what Robert always, without fail, referred to as "our book" in a revised Tenth Anniversary paperback edition; the idea being that, in addition to adding a slew of new articles and reviews, we would update our sagacious saga by including a tribute to Scott Asheton and chronicling James Williamson's return to The Stooges. In contrast to the original edition's polished antiseptic design that was better suited for a trendy upscale travel agency brochure than the roughhouse Stooges, we also agreed that the look of this new softcover should lean toward having a scrappier new veneer that aesthetically evoked more of a '70s rock rag vibe.

One thing we specifically wanted to correct was the opening two page spread that I had personally designed as a tribute to Ron Asheton after his death. My original design had the English translation of Ron's speech set in a bold Germanic typeface. Unfortunately, when the book came out, we were dismayed to see that the "Ladies and gentlemen" text had been inexplicably changed to an ineffectual pencil-thin font that was almost invisible on the page; one which effectively emasculated the original visual intent. This new edition restores those two pages as I originally designed them.

Robert then went through his Stoogefiles to select the photographs that he wanted to use while I compiled a list of the new reviews and articles to be included—but that's as far as we got. Robert's death in 2018 meant that we never had the opportunity to write those updates as we had planned. So that was the end of that, except for the eulogies.

After Robert's death, Iggy told Brian J. Bowe: "Bob was a kind of an extra Stooge. I dunno, the fifth Stooge, the seventh Stooge? The ninth Stooge? Anyway, he showed up at the studio with Scott Asheton one day in '06, and the next thing I knew, we were doing a Stooges photo book. And it was a hell of a good photo history of what the band really was about, because Bob understood us, and who we were. Where we were coming from."

James Williamson seconded that promotion when he told Brian that: "Bob played an important role as a photographer and friend of The Stooges, from the early days through both reunions. Personally, he was always there when I needed photographs or just an ear to listen to and rally my spirits."

I had a eulogy of my own to add. Now that my good friend was gone, it was incumbent upon me to honor both our legacies by completing the interview and photography book that Robert wrote the introduction for prior to his death, *Rock Critic Confidential*. I then followed that book with a second tribute of sorts to another fallen friend of mine, Brian "Renfield" Nelson, when I wrote *Alice Cooper Confidential*.

And then it occurred to me that the time was right thematically to resurrect the reissue that we had planned to produce. Obviously, this is not that book; how could it be with Robert gone? But considering that it contains all of the photographs and texts that we chose, it comes pretty close. And if we never got around to writing those updates about Rock Action and Strait James, well, perhaps it's all for the best. After all, what with *you* being The Stooges' biggest fan, Vegas touts are laying even odds that you could do just as good a job as we ever could, if not a whole lot better.

And as we all know, the Fun House always wins.

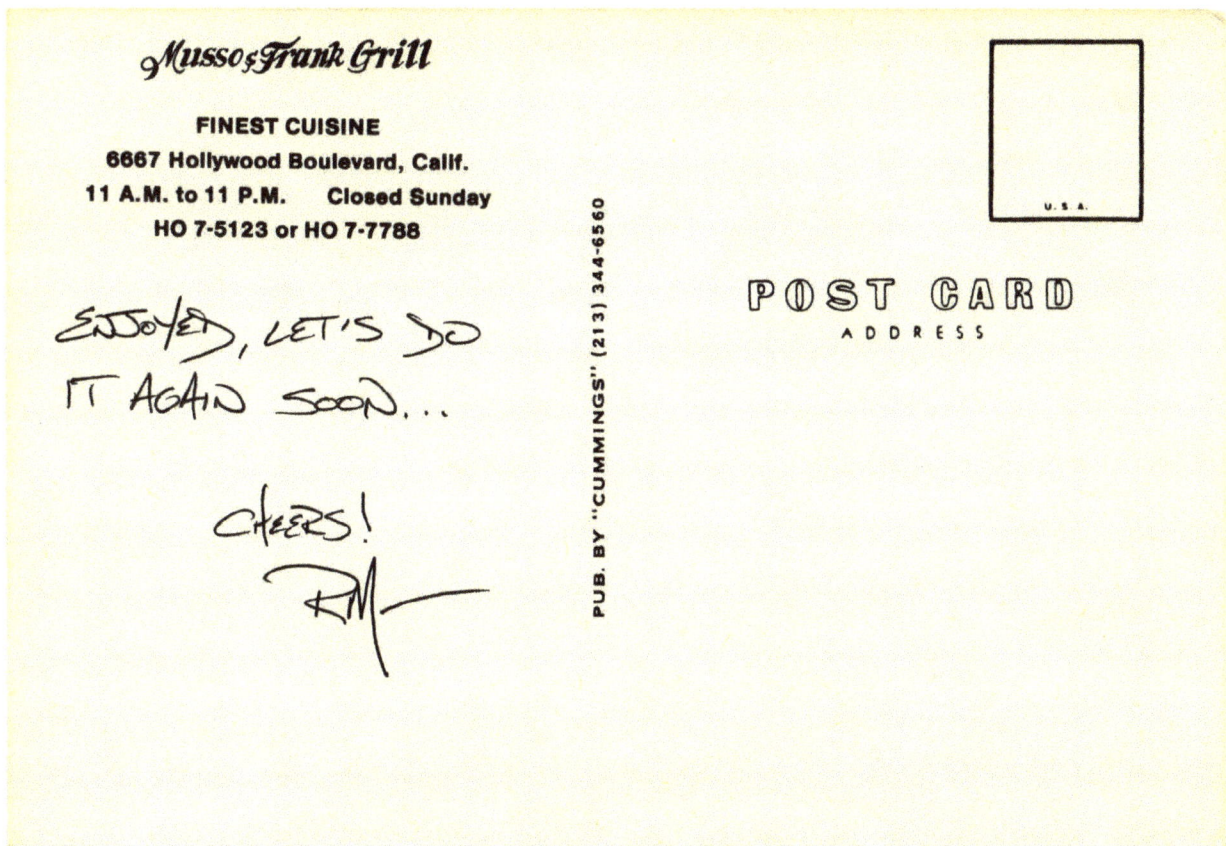

Musso & Frank Grill

FINEST CUISINE
6667 Hollywood Boulevard, Calif.
11 A.M. to 11 P.M.   Closed Sunday
HO 7-5123 or HO 7-7788

ENJOYED, LET'S DO IT AGAIN SOON...

CHEERS!

RM

PUB. BY "CUMMINGS" (213) 344-6560

POST CARD
ADDRESS

U.S.A.

RAW POWER BOOTLEGGER IDENTIFIED!

"Bootlegs are here to stay because the appeal of hearing music that has not been authorized or sanitized by the artist has always been an endearing one. The bootleggers have freed an awful lot of music that the artist themselves might not have 'approved' for release. But then, never trust the artist, trust the tale." — Clinton Heylin, The Great White Wonders, 1994

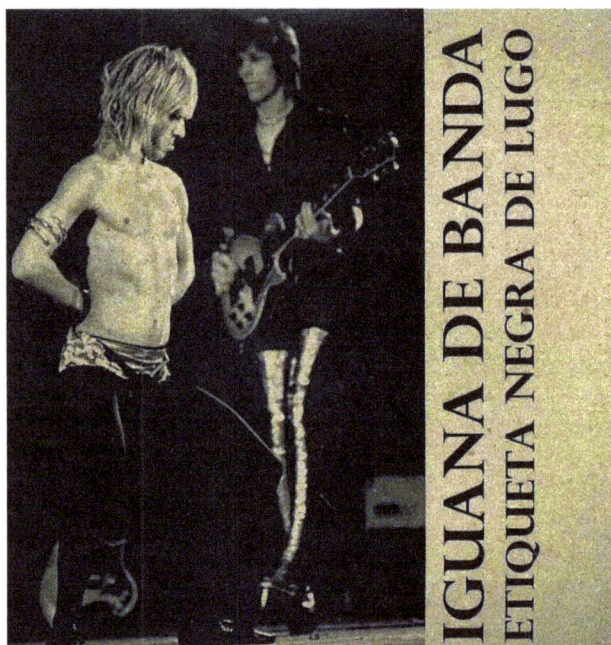

"*iguana de banda - etiqueta negra de lugo* (Boca Del Rey Discos). Limited edition of 1,000. *Raw Power* outtakes. Contains previously unreleased tracks, mixes, and takes. Multiple conspiracy theories exist as to who, where, and why this bootleg was generated." — Discogs

This is rumor control. Here are the facts. Plug me into a lie detector. Strap me on a gurney and spike me with truth serum. Lock me in a room with *Rock Critic Confidential* cover girl Courtney Love. No matter *what* you do, the end result is always guaranteed to be the same because *I* know "who, where, and why this bootleg was generated." Of course I do. Why wouldn't I? After all, not only did the bootlegger personally mail me a physical copy of the vinyl white label edition of *iguana de banda - etiqueta negra de lugo* when it first

came out in 2013 (please note that the lower case album and song titles used throughout are the bootlegger's own nomenclature and not mine), she was also kind enough to include in the same package two additional items.

The first was a flash drive containing the original ten lossless high definition digital masters used in the album's production which, sonically speaking, are far superior to the inferior rips sourced from vinyl that are currently in circulation; the unlisted tenth track being the *a cappella* vocal track "perdo¦ün (ranura interna)."

The second enclosed item was, appropriately enough, a Sony CD-R audio disc hand-labeled "stooges rough real first raw power mixes" containing twelve tracks with a running time of 49:15. The dozen tracks on the disc were, in sequence, heretofore unheard different mixes of "Death Trip," three versions of "Gimme Danger" (all with a drumstick count off by Scott), "Your Pretty Face Is Going To Hell," two versions of "Raw Power," "I Need Somebody," two versions of "Search And Destroy" (the first beginning with a few bass notes from Ron and two power chords from James and a "one, two, three, four" count off from Iggy), "Penetration" (beginning with a few notes from Ron and the engineer saying "Okay" followed by sound of the tape stopping and starting), and "Shake Appeal" (beginning with another "one, two, three, four" count off from Iggy).

Ask me to spin any of these numbers for you the next time you're in the neighborhood and you'll hear for yourself that I *am* telling you the Igg's honest truth when I say that I actually *do* know who's responsible for this infamous *iguana de banda - etiqueta negra de lugo* bootleg. It ain't braggin' if you can back it up, and back it up I most certainly can because now, for the very first time, with her permission for me to do so (under the strict proviso that I not use her real name), I'm now at liberty to finally reveal the heretofore unknown secret story of how these studio quality tracks were made public.

Today she's retired in another country, but back in

2009 Llajta (not her real name) was still working as an executive assistant at Sony Music Entertainment when the *Raw Power Deluxe Edition* was being planned. An inveterate record collector who began buying bootleg albums back in the heady TMOQ and TAKRL heyday of the '70s, longtime Stooges fan Llajta was especially vexed by the same low quality alternate mixes and studio outtakes which seemed to plague every slapdash Stooges boot that she bought.

So when she heard that the original *Raw Power* multi-track master tapes were going to be used in the production of this new box set, Llajta made it her mission to find out just exactly what was *on* those tapes—and the only way she could do that was by obtaining copies of the mixing sessions. After all, she reasoned, if her bootleg hero John Barrett could painstakingly dub The Beatles onto numerous audio cassettes, in real time, back in the '80s, then how hard could it be to do the same thing today, especially when using a fast USB 3.0 transfer speed?

Not wanting to get anyone who still works at Sony in legal trouble, Llajta won't divulge exactly how she managed to physically secure the tracks which appear on *iguana de banda - etiqueta negra de lugo*, but she hints that there was an appalling lapse of security during the filming of an in-studio documentary while Iggy Pop was listening to the multi-tracks and adjusting the faders.

Llajta also coyly suggests that she was able to take advantage of this unguarded area by enlisting the inside assistance of someone whom she knew to be "un admirador secreto de lejos que casualmente era joven y un productor de línea." And although she won't say more than that, the inference is that Llajta convinced this young line producer to dub her a copy of the multi-tracks. Especially since Llajta promised that nobody but her would ever listen to them.

Which held true for several years until she was approached by a record store owner in San Diego who, having heard "penetracion" leaking from her headphones at an indoor flea market, suggested that Llajta allow him to sell a limited edition Stooges album using her rare wares. Recalling all the inferior third generation bootlegs she had to suffer through in the past, Llajta readily agreed and arrangements were made to have the actual records manufactured in Tijuana and then shipped back across the border to San Diego in boxes labeled machine parts. The final step prior to distribution was having the finished discs inserted into the cheap picture sleeves which had also been printed in Tijuana.

At least, that's what Llajta told Robert Matheu after he was surprised to receive a copy of *iguana de banda - etiqueta negra de lugo* in the mail. "Having used my Ford Auditorium photo on the front cover, she felt obligated to send me a copy as payment," Robert laughed after he had related her entire story to me, exactly as she had told it to him. "Anyway, I knew you'd want to hear this, especially the 'all tracks' version of 'potencia en bruto,' so I asked her to put one in the mail for you as well; hope you don't mind. Oh, and now that she's been bitten by the bootleg bug? She wants her next release to be a single of 'hombre de negro' on colored vinyl, but I think I talked her out of it."

Apparently so, but there *is* one mystery about this album that still remains unsolved. The bootleg albums that Robert and I received from Llajta each had a double-sided sheet of paper inside, containing the following anonymous mimeographed liner notes. Were ours the only copies to contain them? Were they too expensive to insert into every copy? How many of the one thousand copies *did* contain one? As far as I know, this is the first time that these liner notes for *iguana de banda - etiqueta negra de lugo* have been made public. The identity of the person who wrote them remains unknown.

*** *** ***

SEIZURE NORTEAMERICANA

por Alfonso Bedoya

¿"Quizá fui, ajá, lo que usted llama actualmente a un soplón, qué"?
— Algodón de Joseph en el Ciudadano Kane, 1941

TOME PARTIDO UNO: RUNNIN' BAJO EN la UN-MEMORIA

Vinieron, vieron, conquistaron — y entonces dejaron. Pero Douglas MacArthur como General, ellos regresaron.

Con el Poder Crudo, Los Soplones regresan con una venganza, exhibiendo toda la ferocidad que los caracteriza en su furioso mejor. El Igg. Nadie lo hace mejor, nadie lo hace, el período. Cuando habla de la mente O, el ojo muy central del universo que abre como un inmenso, estar abierto, chupando estómago, el paso aparte para Los Soplones". — Kaye de Lenny

"La banda acelera más allá de algo que ha sido registrado, o ha sido jugado vive o aún soñado de, en años. Sólo una mente sinceramente diabólica podría haber hecho el mejor álbum del' 70s y Iggy aparentemente lo tienen porque ha resumido todo en ocho canciones". — Pantano de Dave

"El monolito de la edad. Habría dado todos los dientes a tener sólo esa bestia es un doble álbum". — Estallidos de Lester

Esas tres citas no fueron escritas décadas después el polvo se habían asentado y cabezas más frías habían prevalecido, fueron escritos con pasión y precisión en el calor del momento la liberación norteamericana, inicial y poco después Cruda del Poder en febrero de 1973; verdaderamente, el primer dos fue utilizado realmente en el anuncio original de impresión de Registros de

Columbia para el álbum — y para la razón buena:

Nadie lo hace mejor. El mejor álbum del' 70s. Más allá de algo que ha sido registrado en años. Sinceramente diabólico. Regrese con una venganza. En su furioso mejor. Toda la ferocidad. Apárte se. Nadie lo hace, el período.

Esos no son que declaraciones ordinarios hicieron levemente porque ellos no describen un álbum ordinario destinado ser jugado levemente. Más que cualquier otras palabras que han sido escritas subsiguientemente, éstos inicialan comentarios cortan al centro y explican mejor por qué tantas personas alrededor del mundo, tanto ventiladores ardientes como músicos profesionales semejantes, todavía consideran el Poder Crudo para ser la última manifestación de piedra' N' rollo encarna en su más puro y la mayoría de las formas desinhibidas — un álbum creado por cuatro músicos de que fueron poseídos literalmente con una comprensión intuitiva, preternatural y extraña Lo que música rock primitiva es realmente, y Poppiously bendijo con la capacidad innata y la confianza suprema crearalo a voluntad, no importa lo que el costo personal o profesional.

Eso no es un patrimonios malos de dejar, especialmente desde que el Poder Crudo es ni un álbum verdadero de Soplones de empezar con. Para una cosa, si quiere conseguir técnico acerca de ello, a diferencia de su álbum de debut y seguimiento de jazzbo de garde de sabio de idiota prototípico pionero, el Poder Crudo nunca ha sido acreditado oficialmente únicamente a "Los Soplones". De hecho, varios primero copias de edición del Poder Crudo proclamado sólo el contrario extirpando la banda completamente con una acreditación delantera de cobertura que chilló simplemente "IGGY" en gotear grande cartas apropiaron propensamente de El Munsters a través de la original que rezuma logo del mundo la mayoría de los notorios horrores cómicos, los Cuentos de EC De La Cripta — cuales marcas perfeccionan sentido a la luz de invocación de apertura de Iggy en el vestigio del título del álbum.

Menos aparente es sin embargo la base ocultada detrás de esa etiqueta de título de expediente, que fue un regateando remanente intransigente de los primeros días cuando el registro que llegaría a ser que Poder Crudo fue designado originalmente ser el primer Taponazo de Iggy álbum solo en su lugar. Eses Los Soplones

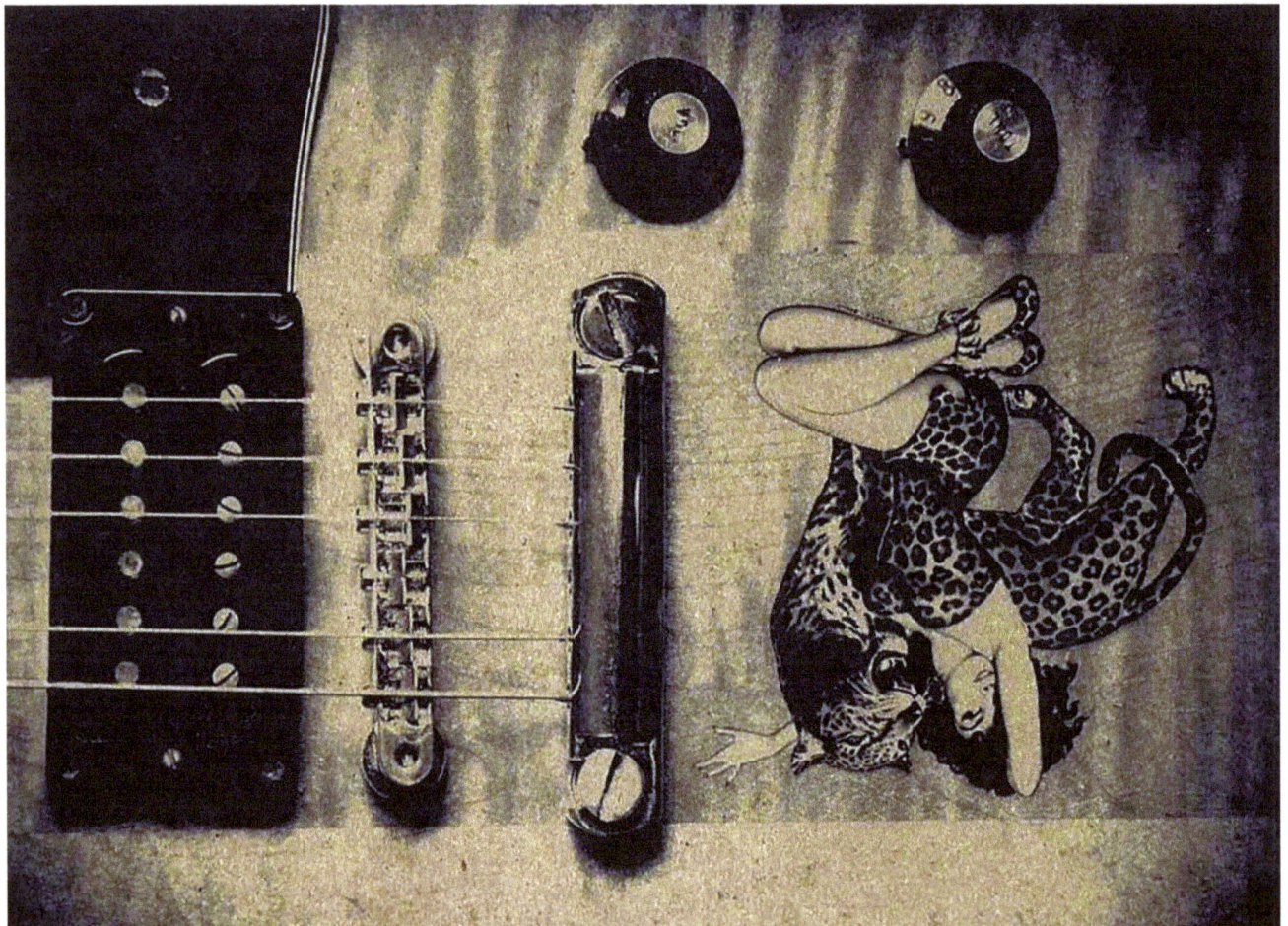

LA SELECCION – BUSQUE Y DESTRUYASE – GIMME PELIGRO

PENETRACION – BUSCAR Y AUTODESTRUCCION

AGITA APELACION – POTENCIA EN BRUTO

NECESITO ALGUIN – MUERTE VIAJE – HOMBRE DE NEGRO

EDICION LIMITADA DE 1000   BOCA DEL REY DISCOS

jugaron aún en ello en todo fue más fuera de necesidad horrible que otra cosa dado que fue El Igg que fue firmado originalmente a MainMan por Tony DeFries, no Los Soplones.

De la importancia mucho más grande es sin embargo el hecho absolutamente crucial que el Poder Crudo no representa Ron Asheton en la guitarra—y no es un axioma invariable que un álbum de "Soplones" sin wah-wah de la firma de Ron en acaba de ser un álbum de Soplones, el hijo.

Entonces si considera fervorosamente la Casa Divertida para ser el mejor álbum de Soplones jamás, las buenas noticias son eso, técnicamente, puede continuar mantener esa creencia, seguro en el conocimiento que usted también puede conceder el Poder Crudo el mismo respeto máximo que demandas enajenadas y ligeramente trastornadas lejanas de pariente. Y no hace error, esto es un álbum muy exigente.

Las mejores noticias uniformes son ese Poder Crudo tiene más de suficientes sangre familiar rociada que encrespa por sus venas obstruidas aseguran que esta oveja negra sea un ejemplar anormal de caballo-dicked de una bestia que nunca acabará en nadie cuarto de baño tomó dosis excesiva y de rodillas. Si piensa que puede vivir con eso, entonces quizá tendrá lo que toma para acercarse con cuidado esta creación aberrante de conjunto fragmentario Frankenstooge y últimamente aceptarlo en los únicos términos que jamás aceptará usted en: su propio. ¿Bastante una escena buena, no es? Una banda loca, cuatro creadores muy sanos.

De manera comprensible, los etnomusicólogos pensaron de otro modo. Después de todo, cualquiera que ha inclinado a sentarse alrededor con un buncha falutin alto' intelectuales académicos elitistas y tener têtes pequeño íntimo de à de tête acerca de los detalles minuciosos arcanos de alguna etiqueta oscura de registro de páramo que nadie jamás es oída de es manera demasiado presumida de levantar el garrote duro-labrado que es el Poder Crudo.

Cuál es de no decir que críticos obreros fueron cualquier más práctico cuando vino al sussing fuera la situación. Aún los adherentes de Igg más astutos, muchos de quien pensaron que sabían la extensión llena de lo que Los Soplones fueron capaces de, nunca recibió el menor aviso previo que algo peligroso arrojaba mortalmente hacia ellos en la velocidad precipitada hasta que fuera demasiado tarde y la máquina de músculo de Ciudad de Motor que retumba tuvo ya smearcased ellos bajo sus ruedas de revista. Ellos nunca supieron qué éxito ellos porque, aumentaron por el Doble Balancín apretadamente enrollaron de Asheton pesado-hemi motor y chispearon por guitarra alta de combustión de Williamson, conductor loco Iggy había aumentado la entrada y excedido todas las esperanzas girándose el fresco lejos el bloquea souped arriba Stoogemobile en la superdirecta e imponiendo un parche que arde que dejó todos emboscado y estrangulándose en su espuma. Pero como cada Rey de Kustom Kulture de Ed "Papá Grande" Roth a George Barris sabe, la transformación del montón de depósito de chatarra al coche sobrecargado del músculo a menudo puede ser un arduo uno — y nada fue más difícil de tratar con que el asunto delicado de "degradación" hipotética de Ron de la guitarra al bajo.

Todavía siempre que el sujeto comenzar a hablar en el pasado, James Williamson, a su crédito eterno, siempre mantuvo fijamente que su decisión de reclutar el una vez y futuro guitarrista de Soplones para jugar bajo en el Poder Crudo fue el correcto. Que él todavía hace hoy es no una tentativa atrasada en retrospectiva valla-reparando en James' la parte, es la opinión aprendido de un hombre que jugó primero guitarra al lado de un bajo que juega Ron Asheton cuando fueron en instituto y miembros de los Pocos Escogidos. Además, como ambos el álbum Crudo del Poder mismo y sobreviviendo subsiguiente vive cintas de visita atestiguan hábilmente, Ron fue sinceramente un bajista excepcionalmente diestro que fue igualmente experto en azotar cuatro picaduras como estuvo en destrozar seis.

Otra razón por qué nadie jamás se opuso indignadamente a Ron Asheton que juega bajo en el Poder Crudo es porque su suplente resultó ser el Roy Hobbs de piedra' N' rollo. James Williamson fue un hasta ahora desconocido "natural" que salió aparentemente de en ningún lugar, ascendió al plato, y entonces continuó para

aplastarlos repetidas veces fuera del parque en la moda espectacular antes de desaparecerse atrás en el éter. No es que James estuvo en ninguna manera un mejor guitarrista que Ron, es sólo que su enfoque entero al instrumento fue tan radicalmente diferente de cómo Ron jugó — y de lo que Los Soplones habían sido utilizados anteriormente a—que ninguna comparación posible del dos fue injustificado.

No hay también negar el hecho inatacable que es James' guitarra desrazonable de almádena que da cuenta en la parte grande para el aguantar enorme de registro y atraer influye. El Poder crudo — y estuvo allí jamás un álbum más propensamente denominado — nunca habría podido vivir de acuerdo para a su título sin su estilo singular de ringlera-cortando que perforó simultáneamente y dio puñetazos. Es un logro asombroso hecho todo el más extraordinario desde que los único otros guitarristas en el planeta en aquel momento que vino aún cierra remotamente a emparejar dedo de James para acatar para tal ferocidad completa, loca y desenfrenada fueron Seña de Jeff y Mick Ronson en Inglaterra — e incluso parecieron un par de pañitos de adorno delicados próximo a los trozos que zarandean de sonido que el James Insurgencia Recto producía penosamente sin descanso. Mientras tanto, atrás en los Estados, su trabajo audaz de hacha fue creído tan radicalmente ronco eso, de manera predeterminada, El Cráneo fue situado universalmente número uno en un campo de uno.

TOME PARTIDO DOS: GOIN' ABAJO EN UN-HISTORIA

Aunque un exceso de descuidada contrabandee Stoogeologists abundado y ardiente fue desconcertado por décadas sobre la escasez horrible de outtakes Crudo de alta calidad de Poder. No estuvo hasta casi el final del último siglo sin embargo que se pareció a sus oraciones de larga duración por último sería contestado. Si 1997 exhumación de audio de Iggy que apareció la música Hola como Fiel puede ir sólo agregó más combustible a su deseo para oír cintas magistrales adicionales, entonces fue la 1999 liberación del conjunto limitado revelador de caja de edición 1970: Las Sesiones Divertidas Completas de la Casa que se inflamaron completamente su estudio salivaciones muertas de hambre. Para después de oír esos siete discos que delinearon definitivamente Los Soplones que registra metodología sobre un período de ocho horas secuenciales, que podría ser culpado para pensar deseosamente que sin duda sólo sería un asunto de tiempo antes que Columbia viera igualmente la luz y soltara 1972: Las Sesiones Completas de Poder de Crudo.

Pero la búsqueda década-largo esmerada para el outtakes Crudo del Poder no es nada comparó al debate décadas-largo doloroso que continuó rabiar sobre la combinación final de registro — una algarabía infernal que ha continuado más de 35 años después del hecho. Y aunque nadie que comprara el álbum en 1973 quiso lo que oyeron, tal es fuerza inexorablemente brutal Cruda de Poder que aporrea que aún la original profirió injurias universalmente "todo el Jim y James, ningún Ronnie ni escocés" combinación pudo no herir el álbum, permitió matanza sola — no que algún no tuvo asesinato en los ojos del primer momento que oyeron la reducción sónica final de vinilo, ninguno más tan que un La Acción colérica de la Piedra que echó la fuente fuera su puerta principal después de escucharlo.

Sin embargo, a riesgo de esta vista general clandestina que llega a ser el Dr. Stoogelove o: Cómo Aprendí a Parar Venerar Y Dejar caer El Taponazo, me conviene indicar que hay varias razones buenas verdaderas en cuanto a por qué la 1973 versión ahora se sienta sólidamente supremo en los corazones y tiene inconvenientes en cuartos de oyentes mundiales; no lo menos de que es El remezcla/remauling muy propio de Igg que proporcionó un marco de referencia mucho necesitado contra que la ofrenda original podría estar retroactivamente Revalorado, con frecuencia con resultados favorables. Podría pasar, así que hago.

Uno podría discutir fácilmente que un componente clave de mentiras perversas Crudas de atracción de Poder en la manera que seduce subliminalmente usted en pensar que todo ocho de sus vestigios de álbum fue registrado y fue mezclado por ocho entidades diferentes con susceptibilidad igualmente divergente. Necesitaría un máster avanzado en la música forense para encontrar cualquier resto de los ataques aéreos tácticos, la espada lucha, y apoyando vocal que es dicho ser enterrado en algún lugar hondo dentro de los límites de su sonido de cal viva que envuelve. Mas a pesar de esta disparidad unificada, la mayor parte de lo que puede ser oído, con poquísimas excepciones, parece de manera incongruente en atrás a mono modo, guarda para el efecto estéreo, anómalo y siniestro de eco o cacerola a través del Canal de la Mancha en que es dejado caer bruscamente. El efecto repentino resultante del golpe es fácilmente el equivalente auricular de Castillo de William insertando inesperadamente gotas gruesas de sangre rojo fuerte en su psychotronic blanquinegro filman El Tingler. Y usted todavía se pregunta por qué hay inscripción de película de monstruo en la cobertura delantera...

Pero cada casa de horrores tiene su acción de accidentes de charnel y el Poder Crudo no es excepción a la persona macabra. No siempre, pero ciertamente las más veces, jugar bajo de Asheton de Ron es certificado criminalmente a MIA, nunca ser encontrada. Y si el tambor logra tener una tasa ligeramente más alta de supervivencia, es único porque Scott Asheton hace repetidas veces una tentativa esforzada de persona enérgica para levantarse fuera

del vórtice que se arremolina para sólo ser echado para atrás abajo. Mientras tanto, el cantante y el guitarrista se pegan en una pendencia descubierto-cedido brutal para supremacía sónica que últimamente terminará con su mundo entero que choca abajo alrededor de ellos, dejando todos enterraron vivo en el cieno.

Mas no sólo hizo el álbum sobrevive, continúa prosperar. Por supuesto hace. ¿Cómo puede no cuando, en un cataclismo singular de convergencia, los Destinos alinearon para asegurar que su letra sea tan mínimamente intuitiva y su maestría musical tan muscularmente inciteful? Y cuán explicar más lo que sucedió en la tarde del 31 de octubre de 1972 cuando un ingeniero de estudio borró por inadvertencia las cintas Crudas de maestro de Poder, sólo encontrar cada vestigio inexplicablemente intacto la mañana muy próxima — como si la música se hubiera reconstituido de algún modo por la noche.

¿Mi amigo, puede demostrar usted que no sucedió?

¿Y se siente usted ese ritmo?

IGGY POP

photographed by Robert Matheu in Chicago
on October 23rd 2006

NEVER BET AGAINST THE STOOGES
by **Robert Matheu**

The Stooges were always there ever since the beginning of time, at least as far as my own personal concert experiences go. And while I might have seen Paul Revere & The Raiders at the Michigan State Fair first, it wasn't long after that when I saw The Stooges on a double bill at the Eastown (or maybe the Grande Ballroom) with Funkadelic (or maybe Alice Cooper). I'm not entirely sure, but it doesn't really matter because either act would've meant being in for some pretty outrageous music, which meant nothing that you ever saw on *The Ed Sullivan Show*, or anywhere else for that matter.

Even the Stones were pretty tame compared to some of the intense stuff I saw at the Grande: Funkadelic sporting diapers onstage and Alice fine-honing his *strum und drag* routine. But when Iggy jumped off the stage right into the crowd we were never sure *what* might happen; all we knew was that we didn't want an angry singer coming at us—and "I Wanna Be Your Dog" sure seemed like he was seriously pissed off about something.

Just like Alice, The Stooges were local mainstays, playing a high school one weekend and the Grande or the Palladium a week later in Birmingham. Years later, one show at the Ford Auditorium still stands out in my Real Mind's Eye as a one of a kind experience that was like nothing we had ever seen before. The crowd that night represented the burgeoning glam movement, only crossed with Detroit "street" values: satin and fishnet, layered with biker leather and boas. But in the end, it really didn't matter what anyone was wearing that night after The Stooges stormed the stage and sliced everyone into psychic shreds with precision dissection.

Rock 'n' roll is riddled with many an improbable story, but the salacious and sagacious saga of The Stooges is truly the unlikeliest of the lot. Forget about your standard boilerplate bio humble beginnings: from their unimaginably impoverished teenage years in Ann Arbor, The Stooges suffered through a seemingly endless series of brutal ups and downs. No other band ever endured more derisive mental and physical abuse, both on stage and off, night after night after night.

I first approached The Stooges with this project over a year ago. There have been countless attempts to document their history, all of them riddled with the oft-told tales of swirling darkness, stumbling missteps, and downright insanity. What we have here instead, however, is an entirely different view altogether: an unabashed *celebration* of a band that started out with no discernible talent yet somehow managed to buck the odds and survive to the point where, after a thirty-four year hiatus from recording, they released *The Weirdness* and triumphantly hit the road where they played to packed houses ever night.

The Stooges have been reunited for some five years now. I've seen almost twenty of their performances since their return and they've never been tighter. The Asheton brothers are an indestructible two-headed monster locked into the "mind-room" while the singer stands on stage, seemingly in utter awe of the band around him. One night backstage, while delivering a post-show mortem, I jokingly told Iggy that he had a pretty tight little band. "No, it's not my band," he said, immediately correcting me. "I'm just a part of this. It's *these* guys . . ." Iggy paused to look across the room at Ron and Scott. "It's *them* driving this thing."

*** *** ***

When I wrote the above six paragraphs as the New Year approached, it was inconceivable that we would ever lose our beloved Stooges guitarist Ron Asheton. He had lived the dream for the last five years of his life; a dream that started as a teenager when his thoughts turned from joining the Marines to honorably serving in The Stooges—and all because he watched George Harrison's band on television in February 1964.

The *Raw Power*-era Stooges, with Ron on bass, played only one infamous gig outside of America on their second tour of duty. But after they reformed, they globetrotted Stoogemania all over the world from England and Europe to Japan and Australia. Yet at the end of each successful campaign, Ron would always return home to Michigan where he enjoyed the simple life: writing music, telling stories, sitting with friends around a campfire, and enjoying a vodka. In those years when The Stooges were MIA, I knew Ron as a warm, easy going, very funny and generous man, friend, and Field Marshall.

In 1969, most people said that The Stooges would never make it. In 2009, a few people *still* steadfastly refuse to recognize the monumental enduring influence that The Stooges have had in the history of rock 'n' roll over the past forty years. Perhaps this book will make believers out of them.

Any bets? Any bets, anyone?

THE STOOGES, YES

by **Robert Matheu** *and* **Jeffrey Morgan**

"When the legend becomes fact, print the legend."
— *The Man Who Shot Liberty Valance*, 1962

Let's face it: from "The greatest rock and roll band in the world!" to "The hottest band in the land!" rock music has been riddled with any number of overly indulgent, self-proclaimed, cheapjack catchphrase stage introductions that are tailor made to set you up and then, inevitably, one day let you down hard. The greatest? Not tonight. The hottest? Not anymore.

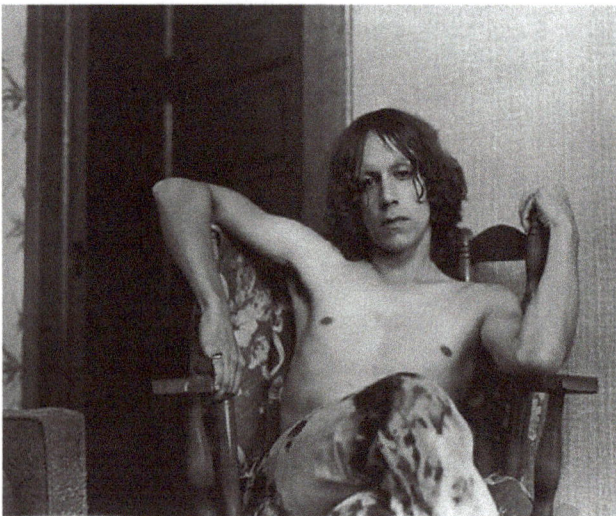

But no truer words were ever uttered before the commencement of a live performance than the ones which Ron Asheton literally *screamed* out on stage at the top of his lungs—in German, no less—over James Williamson's opening sledgehammer riff to "Raw Power" every night on the *Raw Power* tour. You just read them yourself just a few pages back, but they're worth repeating again in the mother tongue because they sum up the very essence of the band we're talking about: "*Damen und Herren, es freut mich sehr, heute Abend, Ihnen ein sehr mächtiges Band, Die Stooges!*" And make no mistake, that emphasis on the key descriptive word "mächtiges" was no fluke. "I have my mad moments of megalomania," Ron reflected to Jymn Parrett in the influential rock 'n' roll fanzine *denim delinquent* after The Stooges had strutted their stuff on the catwalk at the Victory Burlesque Theatre in Toronto

on January 25th, 1974. "Like the introduction to the show. I get off doing that German speech. I *love* doing that!"

If you were lucky enough to have been in the audience for one of those shows, it was a riveting moment you didn't have to wait long for. But even if you *did*, that was quite alright because The Stooges have *always* been worth waiting for, whether it was for three months or for three decades. And if they happened to give us the hard letdown on more than one occasion, well, that was alright as well because they always managed to somehow repeatedly haul themselves up from the crumbling edge of the abyss, scrape themselves off, and start all over again—from scratch. Of course they did. Was there any other choice?

The storied saga of The Stooges has been celebrated both in pictures and in print for over forty years now but, unbelievably, there remain some tight energy emitters who *still* consider Stoogemüsik to be nothing more than an incidental and most unfortunate by-product of their very existence. Such a stubborn lack of respect only goes to show how willfully ignorant some people can spitefully continue to be when confronted with an overwhelming irrefutable truth— namely, that out of some of the most unique circumstances a band ever confronted, The Stooges spawned some of the most unique music a band ever created.

Those of you who have heard this oft-told tale before are cordially invited to push pause and peruse the pretty pictures instead. For those of you who *haven't*, however, we feel it would be a little unkind to go on without just a word of friendly warning. We are about to unfold the story of The Stooges, a band who sought to recreate rock 'n' roll after its own image. It is one of the strangest tales ever told. We think it will thrill you. It may shock you. It may even horrify you. So if any of you feel that you do not care to subject your nerves to such a strain, now's your chance to . . .

Well, we *warned* you.

Once upon a time—we *are* relating a legendary myth, after all; albeit one whose skewed details will forever remain open to debate despite our best efforts to straighten them out in this *Stooges Digest Condensed Book*—four boys from the wilds of eastern Michigan in Ann Arbor and Ypsilanti set out to make an impression. Whether they did it by making the natives restless with their unabashed atonality or by endearing themselves to the scant few who understood their early attempts at performance art really didn't matter, just so long as they left a mark. Preferably a deep one.

As has been mentioned on numerous times in the past, not the least of were made by the subject himself in such subsequent autobiographical songs as "Born In A Trailer" and "Rich Bitch," James Newell Osterberg grew up in a trailer park in Ypsilanti, Michigan. His father was an English teacher at Fordson High School in Dearborn, a bordering suburb of western Detroit. Ron and Scott, the Asheton brothers, grew up in a military family that moved around from Washington to Iowa before finally settling in Ann Arbor in 1964. Their father Ronald Franklin Asheton, who was Ronnie's namesake, had served proudly in the Marines and both Ron and Scott looked up to him with a great deal of respect. Sadly, Mr.

Asheton died a year after they moved to their first house on Creal Drive. Later, the family relocated to a new home on Highlake Avenue.

Scott was a year younger than Ron and younger sister Kathy. When Scott was about to turn ten, he asked his mother for a guitar because his older brother had started to play guitar the year before, having received it as *his* tenth birthday gift. When Scott's mother replied: "No, *you* play the drums; your *brother* plays guitar . . . " it set the tone for what was to follow in their future musical endeavors, with Ronnie always being the big brother; always being the leader.

Several years later, Jim was attending Pioneer High along with the Ashetons when Dave Alexander moved into the brothers' neighborhood one summer, reeking of teenage attitude. Ron and Scott befriended him to the point of asking their Mom if she'd drive them all to their first day of school that September. When the appointed day came, Dave showed up at the Asheton residence reeking of something else entirely: he was rip-roarin' drunk. Nevertheless, all three were dropped off at Pioneer as planned but Dave made it only as far as the foyer before he turned around and walked out, never to return. Realizing that they were also literally too cool for school, both Ashetons would later follow suit.

Meanwhile, Jim had started playing drums in a band called the Iguanas which led to him beating out similar skin sessions in the blues-based Prime Movers where, parenthetically, his former band's name earned him a brand new *sobriquet*: Iggy. By all accounts from those that saw him, the newly-named traps master played a pretty mean Chicago blues shuffle . . . but music wasn't his only mistress. When he wasn't busy applying the brushes, the newly-named Igg was busy brushing up on one of his other passions: ancient history. Long hours were spent studying the lives of everyone and everything from the American Indians to the Egyptian Pharaohs—and who's to say that those noble warriors and golden gods didn't end up having as much of a musical influence on Iggy as Sam Lee did? After all, they *did* show up for work sartorially shirtless, didn't they?

By this time Iggy and Ronnie were already thick as thieves, what with Ron having briefly played with The Igg in the Prime Movers for a short time—and the *reason* why it was for a short time was because it only took a couple of rehearsals before it became painfully apparent that Ron's style of playing was somewhat less than akin to everyone else's notion of what the blues should sound like. Which may or may not have also had something to do with the way Ron played: with his back to the audience, so that he could hear his amp better.

A true blues breaker in more ways than one, the game of musical chores continued with Ron switching over to bass and joining the Chosen Few. Ron always loved to tell the story of how he would later play the intro bass riff of the Rolling Stones' cover of "Everybody Needs Somebody" onstage at the opening night of the Grande Ballroom in 1966, thus baptizing the old Detroit dance hall with its first rock 'n' roll grace notes. It was around this time that Scott, tagging along as a roadie, went to New York with Ron when the Few were auditioning at Columbia Records for a singles deal which never materialized. Scottie materialized at Shea Stadium, however, when he bailed on the band to go see The Beatles.

Back home, it was during one of Ron's gigs at a frat house party that James Williamson, who had recently left the Few himself, first met Iggy, who by that time had left the Movers and gone straight to his good friend Ron Asheton and enlisted him to jump ship and form a new band; their *own* band. Scottie was slated as the front man on blues harp with Iggy on drums and Ronnie bringing it all back home on guitar. Rounding out the retinue was Dave Alexander on bass, even though he couldn't play it very well yet—but since when was technical proficiency ever a prerequisite for playing rock 'n' roll? After only a few jam sessions, however, Ron proclaimed that the lineup needed to be adjusted, with Iggy moving front

30

and center since Scottie was a better drummer than the new front man. Once again, big brother was watching.

From the Jefferson Airplane mansion in San Francisco to the Alice Cooper Group mansion in Connecticut, there have been a number of fabled landmark locations where rock 'n' roll lived—but there was only one place where rock 'n' roll died a million slow painful deaths, only to be reborn again stronger and more powerful than ever before. For unlike their peers' palatial palaces, The Stooges set up shop in a secret sonictarium where rock 'n' roll repeatedly went under the knife and was reinvented via a series of relentless experiments that heralded a new heretofore unheard of hardcore form of sound and fury designed and destined to crush everything in its path once it was unleashed. Some called this laboratory of liberation the Stooge Hall. Others knew it as Stately Stooge Manor. But regardless of whatever whispered name it was fearfully referred to, history would show that from now The Stooges would be callin' from the Fun House!

*** *** ***

Right from the very beginning it was of the utmost importance to these young Stooges that they not just stand there immobile on stage playing like some kinda squares. Not after they saw James Brown, they weren't. One look at Butane James and they knew that they wouldn't just have to *move* on stage, they'd have to make the stage *itself* move. Something hadda be *happenin'*, baby, while the band played on—which is why Iggy set out to shake the concept of what it mean to be a lead singer not just to another level but to a brand *new* level. When the band saw a Doors gig together one night and beheld Jim Morrison jumping off the front of stage and into the crowd to run through the isles, sleigh bells must've gone off in the singer's head. Iggy innately knew that he could do better than that; a lot better. Whether the world be ready for what he had in mind was immaterial. The only thing that mattered to Iggy was that he ditch the archetype and become the architect of a revolutionary new black and blueprint which would forever delineate his new performance persona: that of a squirrelly dervish hurtling through the audience with wreckful abandon—a Frankenstooge creation that Dr. Igg himself would ultimately be both adoring of and appalled by.

Scott: "We went to see the Doors and, after that, he had a need to be in the audience; he didn't want to stand to just stand there. He just told us to turn it up, the power just whipped him into his stage frenzy."

Iggy: "I don't know, maybe I have the soul of an ol' drunk blues man. I'm not sure how that works. There's just something about our music that suggests and drives the way the song is performed. With this music it just gets physical."

When it came to naming the band, once again it was Ron who rose to the occasion by bestowing the first moniker, one which merged their two greatest influences at the time: the well-tempered Harry Partch and the ill-tempered Curly, Larry, and Moe. As Ronnie would repeatedly remark over the years: "We get thrown out of restaurants, the cops are always giving us grief, people try to run us over when we cross the street, we are Stooges alright? And when we did acid, we were Psychedelic Stooges!"

In 2007, Ron told a delighted SXSW audience about a 1969 conference call he was on between mouthpieces for Elektra Records and original Stooge Moe Howard, just to make sure that the band's calling themselves "The Stooges" wouldn't in any way legally infringe on "The Three Stooges" name. "Moe said: 'I don't mind as long as they don't call themselves The Three Stooges!' Click, dial tone. We got the blessing of Moe Howard! I was such a huge fan!"

So huge, in fact, that Ron used to visit and spend time with Moe's old Three Stooges partner Larry Fine, when Larry was in ill health from a stroke and living at a motion picture retirement home. The first time he met Larry, Ron went on and on and on about what The Stooges meant to him and that he was in a band named after them and blah blah blah while Fine listened patiently until Ron finally ran out of breath. Then, just like wheelchair-confined Joseph Cotton did in *Citizen Kane*, Larry leaned forward with a twinkle in his eye and conspiratorially said: "That's real good, Kid. Now listen, the next time you visit can you bring me some good Scotch and cigars?" Which Ron duly did, thus providing the beloved entertainer with some of his last pleasures on Earth. These days it seems that almost everyone and their Uncle Abe gets credit for being the fifth Beatle. But if there ever was a fourth member of The Three Stooges, it was Ron Asheton.

Scott: "When we first started playing together and Jim came around to our house, he told Ronnie and I: 'We're going to start Jim's school of music.'" As might be expected, Jim's school of music was not your typical conservatory. In place of Ludwigs, the Psychedelic Stooges lugged oil drums to gigs and pounded on them with mallets. They took a massive old funnel that they'd found behind the Fun House and performed experiments in feedback by dropping a hot microphone into it while fully amped. Iggy would tap dance with one spiked golf shoe on sheet metal, thus

creating a literal metallic knockout of percussion that even Rock Action found hard to beat. Vacuum cleaners? Blenders through wah-wah pedals? Anything that would create an annoying drone? Oh my, we're gettin' violent.

Early songs would include such charming little ditties as "Asthma Attack," which was nothing less than a frenzied freeform audio assault on the senses. Iggy, who actually *was* asthmatic, would act out the song title by rolling around on the floor, a-yelpin' and a-howlin' all afflicted-like while the band administered sonic resuscitation. At other times, the song might morph into the general malady melody "I'm Sick" or become yet another variation on the always evolving theme "Goodbye Bozos." Then there was the endless coda that went on for half an hour at a stretch. Originally entitled "Dance Of Romance," it would later evolve into "Ann" only with a much shorter length, fading out before Ron's relentless guitar assault. Thus was born the "O Mind" Stoogespeak for letting loose—or as Ron would tell them: "Well, man, just let one go, man. Just let one go."

Iggy really "let one go" one night before an early Psychedelic Stooges show when he decided to shave off his eyebrows, slather Johnson's baby oil all over his mug, and then give himself a full glitter facial. Aside from looking very cool, this little impromptu style

session ended up serving an even greater purpose: it reminded Iggy that his eyebrows were there to keep the stage sweat out of his eyes. Not to mention all of the glittery oil which also cascaded down into his bug-eyed orbs and burned them to the point of blindness.

While the Ashetons were growing up, there was a boy in the neighborhood by the name of Jim Popp. He'd taken sick in his early teens with some sort of rare disease—might've been Alopecia; no one was really sure—but because of it, young Jim Popp had no eyebrows. Years later, those lighthearted lads at the Fun House immediately remembered the O.P. (Original Poppster) the first time they saw the newly eyebrow-less Jim Osterberg. You'll never guess what they called him. But instead of immediately using it as his stage name, Jim opted instead to adopt what would become the most influentially prescient name in the protopunk pantheon: Iggy Stooge.

Iggy: "I play and that's who I am. That's why my name isn't important to me. If I am on the floor, I play. If I'm alone, I play. If I am Iggy Stooge, I play. If I'm Jim Osterberg, I play. I play when I'm popular and when I'm unpopular. I play when I'm happy and I play when I am unhappy. It's as if I'm permanently plugged into the wall. I am plugged in and therefore I play. I have played, I play, I will play."

Pretty soon every band member gained their own *nom de Stooge* which was gleaned through their minds' television eye. From the western *Gunsmoke*, Dave became Dude Arnett. Ron became Cummings after Hitchcock actor and *Love That Bob* star Bob Cummings, whom some thought Ron looked like. Another childhood friend, roadie Bill Cheatham, became Red Rudy; in addition to numerous later Stooge activities, Cheatham would also make a cameo appearance on the *Fun House* box set as wrestling announcer Red Rudy. And last, but certainly not least, Scott Asheton was—and forever will be in the rock and roll hearts of many—the one and only Rock Action.

*** *** ***

When The Stooges were initially signed to Elektra Records, industry *wunderkind* Danny Fields had gone to Michigan to check out the MC5 to offer them a record deal. He saw The Stooges play in April 1968 as well, and offered up both bands to Elektra chairman Jac Holzman. But Danny boy saw something in The Stooges that no one else did; maybe it was the trousers—or in Iggy's case, the sometimes lack thereof. Whatever the reason, when The Stooges were sent packing to wax their debut album in New York, they arrived at La Guardia without a single singable song to their name. Despite all the complications, Holzman teamed the band with another legendary noise boy as their producer: excommunicated Velvet Underground co-conspirator John Cale. The Stooges wrote most of their best songs in Room 101 of the Chelsea Hotel the day before the sessions would start. Then, commencing on the high holiday of their patron saint—April Fools Day of 1969—they then proceeded to record the entire album in only two days at the Hit Factory. But before we continue, perhaps a few words are in order about what makes a good Stooges album cover.

For decades people have wondered why The Stooges' first album cover is an identical ape of The Doors' first album cover. Sure they were on the same record label and, yeah, both bands had four members apiece but, other than that, no one could see the similarity between the two—most of all Iggy Pop, who vehemently hated the cover then and loathes it even more now.

Iggy: "Now Ronnie always corrects me from time to time but, the way *I* remember it, I didn't want to just be posed there because we were a band that *moved*. So I got the other guys on the floor all huddled together and I decided that I'd jump up over them like Evel Knievel going over the fountain at Caesars—and just like Evel, I crashed down on Scottie and went face

first into the cement floor. Scottie was always cool about those things 'cause I crashed into him a lot over the years. So I went to the hospital to get stitched up and came back the next day. I had been smoking some weed by then to ease the pain and I was all swollen up and my eyes were a little puffy so they decided to use the photo that looks like the Doors on the front, cropped above the chin. Then they had to draw in one of my eyes on the back cover because it was closed, ha ha ha. When I finally saw the cover I wished I'd had *both* my eyes closed!

"You see, The Stooges are a very kinetic band on stage but, for some reason, very few photographers have been able to capture what we do on stage in a studio setting—especially in the early days when there weren't too many photos taken of the four of us together. So seeing a nicely posed photo of us looking like every other band in the world always makes me feel like we're dressed up for a funeral of something. I'd personally rather see a photo of the four of us moving or doing something different than just posing there like four wax figures, that kind of thing, which is what everybody else does and it's very boring to look at—and The Stooges are not a boring band. Unfortunately, there aren't too many of those kind of photos around that really convey who we are. But the ones that I've seen are very cool."

Meanwhile, back at Elektra World Headquarters, head honcho Holzman was surprised to find that John Cale—the man responsible for co-writing such hit songs as "The Black Angel's Death Song" and "Sister Ray"—had inexplicably delivered an unacceptable mix that had no commercial potential. So Jacco went back into the studio with future *Raw Power* remixmeister Iggy "I'm usin' technology" Pop by his side and personally remixed the album to attain a more palatable sound. He needn't have bothered. *The Stooges* was released in August 1969 to little acclaim and great distain.

Nevertheless, the New! and Improved! Stooges returned to Detroit as an actual bona fide band with real songs and everything. And even though they'd at first felt forced to accept the major art-inhibiting restrictions of the traditional three minute rock song, those shortened selections on *The Stooges* would eventually encourage the band to expand the format even further on their next endeavor.

Slowly they churned . . . note by note . . . chord by chord. Playing and plotting. Plotting and playing. Ron Asheton in particular would sit in his room and pound along to Jimi Hendrix and The Who for hours on end until he emerged with another original crushing chordal figure that would become a song on the next

album—and in less than six months they'd whipped up the songs that *would* become their next album; one which would reflect Iggy and Ron's increasing interest in the free jazz of John Coltrane and Archie Shepp.

It was in February 1970, at the University Of Michigan's Beaux Arts Ball, that Iggy witnessed a performance by Steve Mackay's sax and drum ensemble Carnal Kitchen. Shortly afterwards, while still under the burning butane influence of a St. James sermon ("Let me in! Let me in!"), The Igg headed downtown to see Mackay—who was holding down Jim's old day job at Discount Records in Ann Arbor—and invite him down to their to pad on Packard to jam. The result was an epochal title track which grew out of a heavy throbber of a bass riff that 'Zander had created and which would end up being the solid anchor that sat submerged at the churning core of their startling new album.

In the early spring of 1970, Elektra Records sent the band to Los Angeles—Hollywood, that is: swimming pools, movie stars—to meet their new producer and start recording their second album. They found lodging at Sandy Koufax's Tropicana Motel on Santa Monica, just a bottle's throw from Elektra Studios on LaCienega. The label had already picked Don Gallucci as their knob boss and culture vulture Ron

Asheton immediately recognized the name, having spent endless afternoons affixed in front of the television. "I said: 'Wait a minute, that name sounds familiar! Isn't that Little Donny of *Don And The Good Times*?' I'd watch him when I got home from school on Dick Clark's show *Where The Action Is*. Donny led the house band after Paul Revere & The Raiders left the show." Even better, it turned out that Little Donny also played keyboards on the Kingsmen's version of "Louie Louie" which, as it turns out, was one of only two vocals that the Iguanas would allow young Jim to sing—even if he *did* have a decidedly bent penchant for ribaldly rewriting the song with his own lewd lyrics.

The recording of *Fun House* commenced on May 11th, 1970 and was approached from a completely different perspective than the first album in that all the songs were, for the most part, performed live in the studio with everyone in the same room, with little or no overdubs. Well over one hundred takes were laid down, with over two dozen of them being different versions of "Loose"—a number which it seems was someone's idea of an eventual single. When The Igg exclaims "Hitsville!" during one such take, you're not sure if he's making a Motown reference or giving his imprimatur of approval to Top Ten inevitability. Either way he was wrong because *Fun House* is nothing less

than a subversive shot of Staxian "Soulsville!" served straight up with a Stoogian twist.

Upon completion of the album, a show was booked at the Whisky A Go Go. They'd already taken a short trip to San Francisco to play the Fillmore shortly after starting the album, but the Whisky gig for all intents and purposes was to get some photos to be used for the album cover. The following day the band reconvened back at the Elektra studios for a more a controlled atmosphere shoot and additional portraits which would then be "double-exposed" with the live shots from the night before. Iggy and Scottie still remember why the session took so long to complete: "Yeah, we were *wondering* why the photographer kept disappearing into the bathroom . . . "

By this time, the suave standard "The Shadow Of Your Smile" was included as a little opening in the set that The Stooges would use as an opportunity for the audience to collectively catch their breaths and let what they'd just witnessed seep deep into their seared brainpans before the band tore into their next three chord auditory assault.

"I was listening to a lot of James Brown and Coltrane at the time," Iggy has explained on numerous occasions. "And what James was coming doing with 'Make It Funky' and 'Say It Loud, I'm Black And I'm

Proud' was a minimal high-steppin' bad ass Back To Africa kind of music—and that definitely upped the ante to the point where I wanted something even badder assed than that."

With the new material for *Fun House* tucked snugly under his imaginary belt, Iggy gained a greater strength onstage. Never physically reticent at the best of times, the new songs now pumped him up to the point where any last remaining vestiges of uncertainty were forever banished as a new fearlessness set in. Quantumly surpassing anything that neither St. James nor St. Jimbo would ever dare *dream* of doing, let along actually *attempt*, The Igg was now taking the whole notion of corporeal liberation through a rock 'n' roll performance light years beyond where he found it. Wearing only a pair of gravity-defying jeans which were strategically shredded so that they hung precariously just above his state line, Iggy's new stage presence was a hyper-kinetic contusion of cathartic chaos.

You had to see it to believe it because there's no safe way to accurately describe this human perpetual motion machine of hideously contorted limp wrists flapping wildly against his chest and on top of his head. No sane way to say how this hot jiggin' jitterbugger jumped 'n' jived from one side of the stage to the other with his knees kiltered all akimbo. No sober way to convey the physically impossible contortions that he self-spasmed himself into with a jelly-boned aplomb that even the great extricating handcuff king Harry Houdini would've been hard pressed to address—but whereas Houdini was famous for accepting challenges from his audience, The Stooges *gave* challenges to *their* audience.

Iggy: "How many men do you see every day who, just when they are confronted with the problem of standing on the face of the Earth with other men, don't know what to do with their hands and arms? You see people walking down the street every day who are in pain because they're being ashamed of what they're doing with their eyes and their hands, who are imbalanced in even a physical sense."

*** *** ***

Management requests that those patrons who can answer the question: "Which road is paved with good intentions?" kindly please refrain from laughing out loud during the following paragraph.

Shortly before *Fun House* came out in August 1970, The Stooges reconvened back in Michigan where they proceeded to live on a macrobiotic diet cooked up by Chef Cummings. Having had an exotic taste of Peru by way of Hollywood, The Stooges decided to await the release of their new album by getting back on a healthy track—which meant swearing off all drugs and alcohol.

Getting back to reality, The Stooges were booked to perform at the Goose Lake Music Festival, where they'd play to their largest audience ever alongside a diverse array of talent ranging from Jethro Tull and Faces to Joe Cocker and Mountain to Chicago and Ten Years After. Along with The Stooges, the Michigan contingency was also well represented on stage by the likes of Mitch Ryder, MC5, SRC, and Brownsville Station.

Getting away from reality, The Stooges were less represented on stage by bassist Dave Alexander who was so mentally and physically incapacitated that, immediately after performing to an estimated quarter of a million people, Iggy stormed backstage and summarily fired 'Zander on the spot. Given that the band had already been recently rehearsing without him due to similar lapses, it's a move that probably came as no surprise to anyone—except perhaps Dave.

Ron: "Dave showed up with his girlfriend and he was so overwhelmed by all of it, he ended up drinking whiskey and smoking too much hash after abstaining

for months. He was just so stoned and freaked out that when the stage turned around and there were those hundreds of thousands of people, he kinda froze like a deer in headlights. Right off the bat, he forgot the songs. He was so out of it he couldn't even play."

And as if *that* weren't bad enough, while the band was busy in the dressing room consoling themselves with some post-performance pot, the local constabulary was busy pounding on their door with arrest threats for inciting a riot. It seems that Iggy's repetitive cries of "No walls! No walls!" during "Down On The Street" had been construed as a command to tear down the fences which had been set up in front of the stage. But at least Iggy was shouting in English: one shudders to think of how Wagnerian Ron would have addressed such gathered masses had he stood before them three years later on die *Rohe Energie* tour . . .

Their next shows less than ten days later was at a series of *Fun House* record release parties held at Ungano's nightclub in New York, with roadie Zeke Zettner on bass and "Red Rudy" Cheatham on second guitar. Performing two sets per night, the set list was the full *Fun House* album performed pretty much in its entirely from start to finish. Once again lending credence to the theory that The Stooges had intended for it to begin the album and be the eventual single, they opened up with "Loose" in place of "Down On The Street" and closed down with an extended "O Mind" freak out of "1970 / Fun House / Mindroom." not unlike the modern day medley seen during the 2003 - 2008 reunion sets. Then again, The Stooges themselves have said that they *might* have closed the show with a free form jam entitled "Have Some Fun" with Steve Mackay doing what we all know he does best: playing Stooges sax—except, of course, for that one time when he filled in for an injured Rock Action and played Stooges *drums* . . .

Steve: "Scott and the crew drove a twelve-foot U-Haul under the Washington Street railroad bridge in Ann Arbor (max headroom: 10' 6") and we were all lucky to survive the impact with nothing but split lips and broken noses. I got a call from the band the next day saying that they had a gig at the Eastown and I remember that I had played drums at a rehearsal once in TriBeCa when Scott had gone missing. So I went over to Stooge Manor and tapped out some beats on the top of a practice amp up in Jim's apartment with him supervising: 'That's fine, that's fine, next!'

"The gig itself was more of a nightmare with Jim taking the sticks out of my hand on every song and showing me what he wanted, which I then produced. I hadn't bothered to reset the drums to my body so ended up with a big bruise on my thigh; one of the stage crew from the Eastown said: 'Don't worry Steve, this will be the hardest gig you'll ever play,' and he was probably right! Meanwhile, the crowd was yelling at Jim: 'Come Iggy, let's see you puke!' But I *did* get 50 bucks for the gig . . . " Who *says* this guy's "Not A Stooge"?

(Note from James Williamson: "The chronology of these events is a little off. By the time this truck accident happened, I was already in the band as rhythm guitarist. Steve didn't have any advance notice, as I recall it. He simply jumped up when Iggy asked if anyone could play drums and knew our songs. Of course he didn't, but he was game to try. The whole night was a disaster, with Iggy stopping him constantly to show him how to drum on our songs. Anyway, he was right about one thing. We *did* get paid.")

And speaking of horn-honkers, no less a personage than Miles Davis attended one of the late Ungano's show—at least, that's what *Iggy* says he was told. *Steve* says he saw Miles at the show with his fingers in his ears. *Ron* says that Miles came backstage and had his fingers in The Stooges' stash. *Others* say that there was a backstage "dust up" of epic proportions that night, with Miles playing the generous guest and The Igg yelling: "Miles! Blow!" But whatever else may have transpired that night, there's no denying the connection between what The Stooges were doing on *Fun House* and what Miles ended up doing on *Dark Magus* and *On The Corner*. What do *you* say?

In the meantime, which was a groovy time, the still-burgeoning underground press was having *their* say in spades and the mainstream press wasn't about to be left out. Which is how it came to pass that Mr. Iggy Pop was photographed for *Vogue* magazine, if you can believe that—and you'd *better* because we've got the pictures to prove it. But since a picture's only worth a thousand words, here are forty more as originally printed in *Vogue*'s Spring 1971 number:

People Are Talking About . . .

Iggy Stooge, 23, the wide-toothed, rock-freak singer with a Froggy-The-Gremlin voice. In silver lamé opera gloves and faded jeans, Iggy taunts and worries the audience with his drive and hype: "I wanna be your dog."

*** *** ***

After the Ungano's gigs The Stooges, who had already begun writing new audience-worryin' songs for their next album, headed home to Ann Arbor where another old friend was waiting for them. James Williamson had finished attending night school to obtain his Grade 12 diploma and was looking for something to do with his spare time, so he decided on the spur of the moment to drive all the way up from Detroit to see his freak-rockin' friends. He needn't have bothered. Faced with the prospect of an empty Stoogehaüs and not knowing when the band would return, James did what any other self-respecting Michigan lad would do under the circumstances: he took advantage of an unlocked window and made himself at home.

Eventually Williamson moved to Ann Arbor and, since Ron wanted to keep the two guitar line up which had been established at Ungano's "to free me up from having to fill up the sound on my own," they started jamming and working up some new songs: "I Got A Right" and "You Don't Want My Name" being two of the first. Although Bill was a good friend, he just didn't have what it took to fill the second seat guitar in Stoogeland. It's also around this time that Jimmy Recca stepped in to replace Zeke on bass.

James' first gig with The Stooges would be at Farmington High School on Saturday December 5th, with another gig following a week later at the Palladium in Birmingham. Gone was Mackay and the free jazz stylings of *Fun House*. As Steve explains: "It was with a sense of relief when I got The Call saying: 'We're changing our direction.' I said: 'Happy to have been on your adventure, see you around town.' So I got my old job back at Discount Records where Jim had previously worked. I always stayed on good relations with him and the boys, although it would be many years until I got The Call again saying: 'Welcome back!' "

Now powered by the formidable twin guitar torrent of Asheton and Williamson, the new Stooges sound was literally a lean, mean fighting machine in every sense of the word. Iggy, Scott, Zeke, and James all moved temporarily into a downtown Ann Arbor high-rise apartment to further explore their widening interest in extracurricular activities. away from Ron's well-meaning but nevertheless stifling Mother Hen grasp.

By early 1971, The Stooges' set would consist of all new songs including: "Nigger Man," "Fresh Rag," and "Good Bye Betsy," which would later become "I'm Sick Of You." It's to their everlasting credit that The Stooges never rested on their laurels and traded on their past achievements to attain future fame. Always unwilling to continually grind out "old" songs from their studio albums, they instead jumped headfirst into the future where they would constantly reinvent themselves. It's a confident work aesthetic that the singer in particular would never lose; that's why, unlike so many of his contemporaries who were content to rewrite old material, Iggy never recycled any unused Stooges songs on his solo albums. There were no rear view mirrors on the supercharged Stoogemobile and there definitely was no reverse; just full, flat out, maximum overdrive forward.

Since Elektra Records was sorely disappointed with the grim sales of *Fun House*, which didn't even sell as well as the debut record, it was decided that The Stooges should try and make amends by impressing a few over-assistant West Coast promotion suits. By the time Elektra's Bill Harvey and *Fun House* producer Little Donny Gallucci came to visit the band on their home turf, Ron had taken to locking himself into his second floor "apartment" within the house. It seems that the other Stooges weren't smitten with Ron's spit and polish clean living regimen, nor with him having become the "straight" man to the rest of their ever increasing stooge-like behavior. But if the havoc that ruled the roost at that point wasn't enough to turn off the button-downs, the one thing that *did* make these

babies reconsider was when they went into Ron's room one day and saw his vintage collection of . . . The whole, the whole place was . . . Well it's, it's too horrible to describe. Dreadful. We won't dwell upon it—but Elektra obviously did because it wasn't long before The Stooges found themselves without a recording contract or a record label.

Once again The Stooges headed to New York for a couple of gigs at the Electric Circus on St. Mark's Place and once again Iggy decided to glitter his face for the occasion. Always one to learn from his past mistakes, Mr. Pop was smart enough this time around not to repeat his earlier application error. This time around there would be no sweaty glittery oil cascading down to blind him. This time around Iggy took a can of Testors silver spray paint, closed his eyes, and aerosoled himself.

Lester Bangs once referred to the "Luck Of The Stooges" and he wasn't just whistling in Dixie 'cause the debilitating hits just kept on comin'. As noted earlier, Scottie rammed their crammed equipment truck into a low bridge before a Detroit show which turned him into Rock Inaction and forced Steve Mackay temporarily back into the fold as The Stooges' drummer. Then a gig in St. Louis had to be cancelled because their gear didn't make it to the venue on time.

But the most ignominious incident of all came when the "pseudo-Stooges" had to play their final concert without either James Williamson on guitar, who was seriously sick physically; and without Iggy Pop on vocals, who was seriously sick of The Stooges.

Iggy: "It was getting to the point that I didn't want to appear under that sort of handicap because the band in general was not inclined towards any sort of positive discipline."

With James laying low and on the mend in Michigan, The Igg headed to New York ostensibly in search of other career possibilities. Showing the kind of "positive discipline" that made Michigan famous, he ended up instead spending most of his time at Danny Fields' apartment, watching old Jimmy Stewart movies on the Late Late Show. And *that*, boys and girls, is the end of The Stooges' story.

*** *** ***

At least it *would* have been, had it not been for the timely intervention of David Bowie, a British musician with a decidedly perverse penchant for reviving the careers of recently deceased combos, who opted to use his Lazarus-like come-hither hoodoo to salvage his "favorite singer" at the time, couch potato Pop. Having already successfully resuscitated the

lukewarm legacies of a select few outfits on life support such as Mott The Hoople, that old Bowie magic was on the case like speed on Lou Reed. A few strategically placed beguilingly batted eyelashes later and Iggy was "A MainMan Artiste," exclusively managed by Tony Defries; personally signed to Columbia by head honcho Clive Davis; and leaving on a jet plane for England with newly recovered dizz-buster James Williamson in tow, to search for a mighty Blighty rhythm section heavy enough to shoulder the worthy mantle of Stooge.

They needn't have bothered. Finding the potential pickings a tad on the twee side, Iggy placed a transatlantic call to the all-American Asheton brothers, who flew over only to find that guitarist Ron had now become bassist Ron since the six string position was already filled by James. This perceived "demotion" seeded a series of deep-seated interrelated grudges which, some say, continue to fester to this very day. Understandably, it's at this point in the proceedings that the official narrative gets bogged down in a churning glut of bitter recriminations and still outstanding grievances which differ in degree depending on who you talk to and what time of day it is. You could look it up—and I'm afraid you'll have to since we have no intention of dishing the dirt around here. Well, not *too* much of it anyway.

James: "We were working pretty hard when we were in London and when we weren't working, we were occupied looking for chicks. The only bands that I can recall going to see were T. Rex—Jim and I were both amazed at the adulation of the crowd—and later we saw David Bowie a couple of times and weren't impressed. Other than that, I don't recall any shows that we went to."

After spending May and June in the studio studiously renovating the songs they'd bought over, The Stooges played their one and only show in England: a memorable July concert at London's King's Cross Cinema which had the decidedly belatedly effect of inspiring everyone who was in the audience to start a ground-breaking band of their own within a scant few years—thus making The Stooges single-handedly responsible for spawning the entire epochal senses-shattering world wide punk revolution. Well, *almost* everyone was enamored by what they'd seen and heard: a somewhat less than enthralled MainManagement decided that the songs which The Stooges had demoed were "too subversive," and summarily ordered the band to write new ones which had more commercial potential.

And because they were ever-obliging team players who knew that there was no "i" in "Stooge," the boys eagerly hunkered down and studiously applied themselves to the task at hand with the end result being that, a mere six weeks later, they had written *and* recorded a brand new album chock full of modern day standards which would set the world reeling—an impressive accomplishment that only goes to show what you can do if you really put your mind to it. And although one song stubbornly remained from the original rejected sessions, even then The Stooges were accommodating enough to rename it "Your Pretty Face Is Going To Hell" so that it would fit in snugly with the seven other nuanced song titles.

Iggy: "If memory serves, we only did six to twelve takes of each song as opposed to the dozens we did on *Fun House* because we were much better rehearsed for *Raw Power*. In other words, nobody was gonna make a mistake. When I did the remix, I'd heard everything from Bowie saying: 'There were only three tracks, *what could I do?*' to the engineers saying: 'They put everything on one . . . we didn't even *use* tracks!' Actually, it was a sixteen track recording done on thirteen tracks. There are thirteen clean tracks on *Raw Power*."

With the recording finished, The Igg headed for Los Angeles with James and the others following not far behind. The band then set up Stooge Manor West in

the hills of Hollywood where Mr. Williamson picks up the story:

James: "After *Raw Power* was finished, Iggy went over first. Then Scott, Ron, and I went to Ann Arbor briefly with Angie Bowie—maybe a week at most—and then Angie and I went out to Los Angeles. During this time, Jim and I stayed at the Beverley Hills Hotel. After several weeks of this, MainMan found us a house on Torreyson Drive in the Hollywood Hills. Once we had the house, we then sent for the others to come out to L.A. Yes, there was too much time between then and the Ford Auditorium show, but MainMan was busy with Bowie and we were just practicing . . . up to no good. I was at several of the mixing sessions when Bowie mixed *Raw Power*, and Iggy was too."

Exactly whose idea it was to have David come in and do the final mix has never been clear, even in recent years—and still isn't. Clive Davis himself has taken credit for this supposed stroke of genius, stating that he was so pleased with the success of the Bowie-helmed *All The Young Dudes* album by Mott The Hoople that he hoped to continue that success with what young David could bring to The Stooges. When asked whether it was Columbia or Tony Defries who rejected Iggy's first mix of the album, the singer finally sets the record straight:

"The whole project, as *I* remember . . . if it was Columbia, then it was Defries who told me. But I would say Defries. I had no contact at anytime with anyone from the record company, *ever*. We were signed to MainMan in effect and it was the classic production contract exploitation situation. We didn't have a record contract, we *thought* we did because we were ignorant of the business. In fact, *he* had a contract with Columbia to deliver the zombie—being *me* and any band I was in.

"I met Clive Davis *once* and I think he just wanted to get me outta the office. He picked us up because he passed on David Bowie. *That's* what happened. He passed on David Bowie, realized his error, and what an exec does *then* . . . it makes him very liable to pick up another act by the same manager so you can say you were *involved* in the general movement."

*** *** ***

A grand coming out party was planned whereby the conquering heroes would return to Detroit's Ford Auditorium in late March and once and for all take was what rightfully theirs. James suggested getting ex-Prime Mover Bob Scheff to join them on piano for the gig and they began rehearsing extensively to prepare for the show. They also continued to write new songs which would eventually see the light of day some ten to twenty years after the fact. As their Stoogeography

ably attests, no other band has ever seen so many of their songs released over and over again on "boutique" labels after their demise as The Stooges did—and no other band ever will.

Having been bitten by the commercial songwriting bug, early 1973 saw a surfeit of catchy new numbers suddenly appear on the Stoogescene in locust-like rapid succession. We're talkin' sure-fire crowd pleasers like "Rubber Legs," "Open Up And Bleed," and the ever-popular Stooge Pan Alley standard "Rich Bitch." Them there Stooges may have been many things to many people, but no one *ever* accused them of being slack-jaw slouches in the creative cranium department. Why, just between the recording and release of *Raw Power*, these ardent over-achievers had a dozen brand spanking *new* songs rip-roarin' and ready to go!

And, boy howdy, did they *ever* go when the boys hit the boards at the Ford in a welcomed return to dominant form. Sure they were on stage for less than an hour, but that's all the time it took for The Stooges to re-establish themselves as both the singular irresistible force *and* the immoveable object of all rock 'n' roll. And judging from the adoring audience response, it looked like they were finally getting the respect they deserved. But looks can be deceiving 'cause later that night the band wasn't allowed entry into their own after show party! The Asheton brothers especially were treated like second class citizens in the MainMan world to the point where they had to sneak out just a couple of lousy beers "like hobos on the run," as Ron puts it. It was an ominous omen of things to come.

The band returned once again to Hollywood and lived off a piddling allowance until, finally, management had enough and James was fired by the band for butting heads one too many times. After he filed for unemployment insurance, Williamson went to work at the Projection Room theatre on Western Avenue where he ran porn films all afternoon. One minute he was playing music for wankers, the next he was showing films for them: "Yeah, it *was* a real wanker place but interesting in a very sad sociological sense," James recalls. "But I did get a pretty good sex education in the bargain!" It was during this leave of absence from the band that The Stooges played one gig with Tornado Turner filling in before The Skull was asked to rejoin. And since Scheff had freaked out in a Stoogeage nightmare by all the extracurricular activities that the band had taken on as an ever-growing pastime, when James rejoined he brought along a new ivory tinkler: Scott Thurston, whom he had met at a Capitol Records recording session.

*** *** ***

Red Rudy. Tornado Turner. The Skull. These kind of fight night nicknames straight outta Nat Fleischer's *The Ring* or Bert Randolph Sugar's *Boxing Illustrated* would prove to be a solid staple of Stoogelife throughout the years. Indeed, over thirty years later, The Igg would draw on them every night as he introduced the band like a tuxedoed Vegas ring announcer:

"It's time for the motherfuckin' Main Event! In this corner, on bass guitar, weighing 145 pounds, outta San Pedro, California, The Minuteman, Smokin' Mike Watt!"

"The King Of Beasts, on the drums, 184 pounds of undefeated fighter, The Powerhouse, the baddest criminal in The Stooges, Rock Action!"

"In this corner, from the Motor City, on lead guitar and general confusion, weighing in today at 218, the undisputed Heavyweight Champion Of The World, Ron Asheton!"

"And I'm motherfucking Iggy Pop! And I *love* this fuckin' place!"

However, The King Of Beasts understandably took umbrage in 2005 at the Leeds Festival when motherfucking Iggy Pop introduced him thusly: "On drums, *from the deepest, darkest, unknown regions up my ass . . .* " Okay, we'll let The Powerhouse take it from here:

Scott: "Mike Watt told me about it afterwards. I didn't hear it onstage but I remember Ronnie looking over at me with the expression on his face saying: '*Whaaaaat?*' You know that expression: '*Whaaaaat?*' Jim's intros were always off the wall but *that* one was the *most* off the wall. Ronnie looked at me and I looked back and: '*Whaaaaat?*' I remember Ronnie's face."

So Iggy comes into the band's dressing room with his usual glass of post-gig Bordeaux and Rock Action is still sitting in the corner, toweling off. He then slowly starts to take off his gloves and, without looking up, says: "So . . . Jim . . . what was up with that intro?"

Scott: "That's all I said and then after that I really didn't think anything about it. You know, it wasn't like: 'This motherfucker, I'm gonna kick his ass . . . ' But the next gig, I noticed that he went back to calling me 'The baddest criminal in The Stooges.' And Ronnie was *always* introduced as 'The Heavyweight Champion Of The World.' "

But back in 1973, The Stooges' only introduction was:

"Let's get ready to stumble . . . "

42

And stumble they did when they went back to New York for a series of four gigs that saw Iggy self-inflicting himself with a broken glass stem which resulted in injuries so severe that the last two shows had to be postponed. August through October saw the band blazing through a couple of dozen performances and, for once, all the band members were in agreement that the week-long series of shows at Richards' club in Atlanta were some of the best gigs that they'd played during this time period—and as the Luck Of The Stooges would have it, a new fan of the band just happened to show up for one of them.

Elton John had recently started his own Rocket Records label around this time and was currently basking in the reflected glow of several chart-topping hits by such RR artists as Kiki Dee and Neil Sedaka. And so it was that, flush with success and always up for a giggle, the budding record executive decided to go on a scouting mission and see for himself if these here Stooges that he'd heard so much about had the primo potential to become Rocket men. Elton also thought that he'd have a little fun on the side by making an unannounced onstage cameo appearance. On Halloween night. Right in the middle of a song. While dressed from head to toe in a big furry gorilla suit. And, of course, completely unaware that the singer whose domain he was about to trespass on was, in fact, tripping heavily while under the influence of an extremely potent self-prescribed mind-altering substance.

Medical professionals are still divided as to whether The Igg has ever fully recovered from the psychotronic shock of seeing a giant gorilla heading his way across the stage that night. But everyone is united in the opinion that Mighty Reg Young should *still* consider himself extremely lucky that he didn't get his big hairy ape head repeatedly pounded senseless into the stage by, you guessed it, the baddest criminal in The Stooges who was already halfway over his drum kit to protect Iggy when Elton unmasked just in time to save himself from a serious beating. And you wonder why "Jesus Loves The Stooges" never appeared as a Rocket Records single . . .

Yet another Atlanta show has the distinction of being captured on the only professionally recorded live Stooges stereo multi-track tape in existence. On it, Iggy is heard genially disagreeing with a hapless audience member who had the temerity to editorially shout out: "Your band's shit!" after the opening number. With The Stooges' honor at stake, Iggy immediately steps to the front of the stage and, repeatedly punching the microphone stand to punctuate each point, proceeds to address the matter using the practiced representational argument of the professional debater: "Hey, you wanna get your little *fuckin'* face punched out, little Cracker boy? Come up here! *Come up here little Billy Boy, I'm* sick *of your shit!* Get up here where a man can be seen! *Daddy's pretty little face.* Suck my *ass*, Blueboy." When his opponent doesn't answer the bell to retort, Iggy fittingly introduces "Gimme Danger" as the next number.

But there's a big difference between someone being hapless and someone being helpless, which is why this very same confrontational tactic will backfire on him in spades at the Rock & Roll Farm in Wayne, Michigan where The Igg will learn the hard way that you can't say things about people's mothers from the stage—at least, not to a roomful of bikers you can't. And thus began The Stooges' slow inexorable death crawl that would ultimately culminate in Detroit Stooge City with their final truly legendary show at the Michigan Palace. And while you might look to *Metallic K.O.* for a suitable sign-off, it's on that lone multi-track recording from Atlanta that the singer himself provides the final fitting epitaph for his band's headstone: "It'll all be over soon, Ladies and Gentlemen. It doesn't hurt much after the injection."

*** *** ***

In 1951, General Douglas MacArthur made a speech before a joint session of the United States Congress during which he said: "I still remember the refrain of one of the most popular barracks ballads of that day which proclaimed most proudly that old soldiers never die; they just fade away." And so it was with The Stooges. Not knowing that they'd already played their last gig and were now a Dead Band Walking, they all headed back to Los Angeles where they moved into the Coronet apartment building on Sunset Boulevard for a short while until, just like The Beatles and the Alice Cooper Group before them, each member ended up drifting off, with The Stooges having never officially disbanded.

Snap. What happened to Scott? Aw, he ended up crashing at James and Iggy's place 'cause Ronnie wouldn't allow his own brother to invade the sanctity of his "clean" apartment; besides, there were all those messy extracurricular activities to contend with.

For his part, Iggy made a few guest appearances performing with Ray Manzarek in one-off jams that the press wishfully reported as Doors reunion rehearsals. Sure they tried to form a band but, as Ray referenced: "He'd walk into rehearsal stark naked and the other musicians were just shocked!" And then there was the time that Herr Asheton took Iggy for a ride to Rodney Bingenheimer's English Disco with a pick up band, only to end up whipping his bloodied singer into doggie submission.

Officially billed as either "The Murder Of A Virgin" or "The Sacrifice Of The Virgin Mary" depending on which program you received from the usherette as you took your seat, it seems that the purpose of the performance was to be a self-inflected exorcism in which the monster known as Iggy Pop would finally be killed off—at least metaphorically, although some in the shocked crowd wondered if they weren't witnessing an actual attempted murder. Either way, the event only added more gristle to the ever growing legend of Iggy Pop: Professional Madman.

Say, did you ever hear the rumor that Iggy had the part of his brain that received pain impulses surgically removed? And hey, how about that "Death Of Glitter" debacle at the Hollywood Palladium when Iggy and Keith Moon both dusted up and then proceeded to saddle up? Boy I wanna tell ya, ain't that something? You want Iggy stories? We got a *million* of 'em! And each and every single last one of them has the same sad punch line: namely, that the great Iggy Pop had finally turned into the crazy fool that all his detractors had originally claimed he was; that Iggy Pop was now known more for his embarrassing antics than for his energetic music.

And *that*, boys and girls, really *is* the end of The Stooges' story.

*** *** ***

Not only was this the no foolin' end of The Stooges, it was also the end of Jim's frayed rope—which also meant the end of Iggy Pop as we knew him. Now on the verge of *really* becoming the World's Forgotten Boy, Jim finally found solace in retirement at a local health facility. James Williamson would periodically drop by and together they'd go to Jimmy Webb's home studio and record some demos in the hope that Elton John might still find what Jim had to say interesting enough to warrant a Rocket Records release. They needn't have bothered. The tapes of what would eventually be released years later as *Kill City* ended up languishing on the shelf as yet another noble experiment that failed.

David Bowie also visited Jim in the facility and eventually took him along as a travelling companion on his *Station To Station* world tour of 1976. After that, The Igg and The Zigg would spend well over a year in tandem, recording and touring together in support of the first of the two solo albums which many feel are the two finest examples of Iggy's solo years: *The Idiot* and *Lust For Life*.

Over the next three decades, Iggy would release over a dozen albums—and you can double that amount if

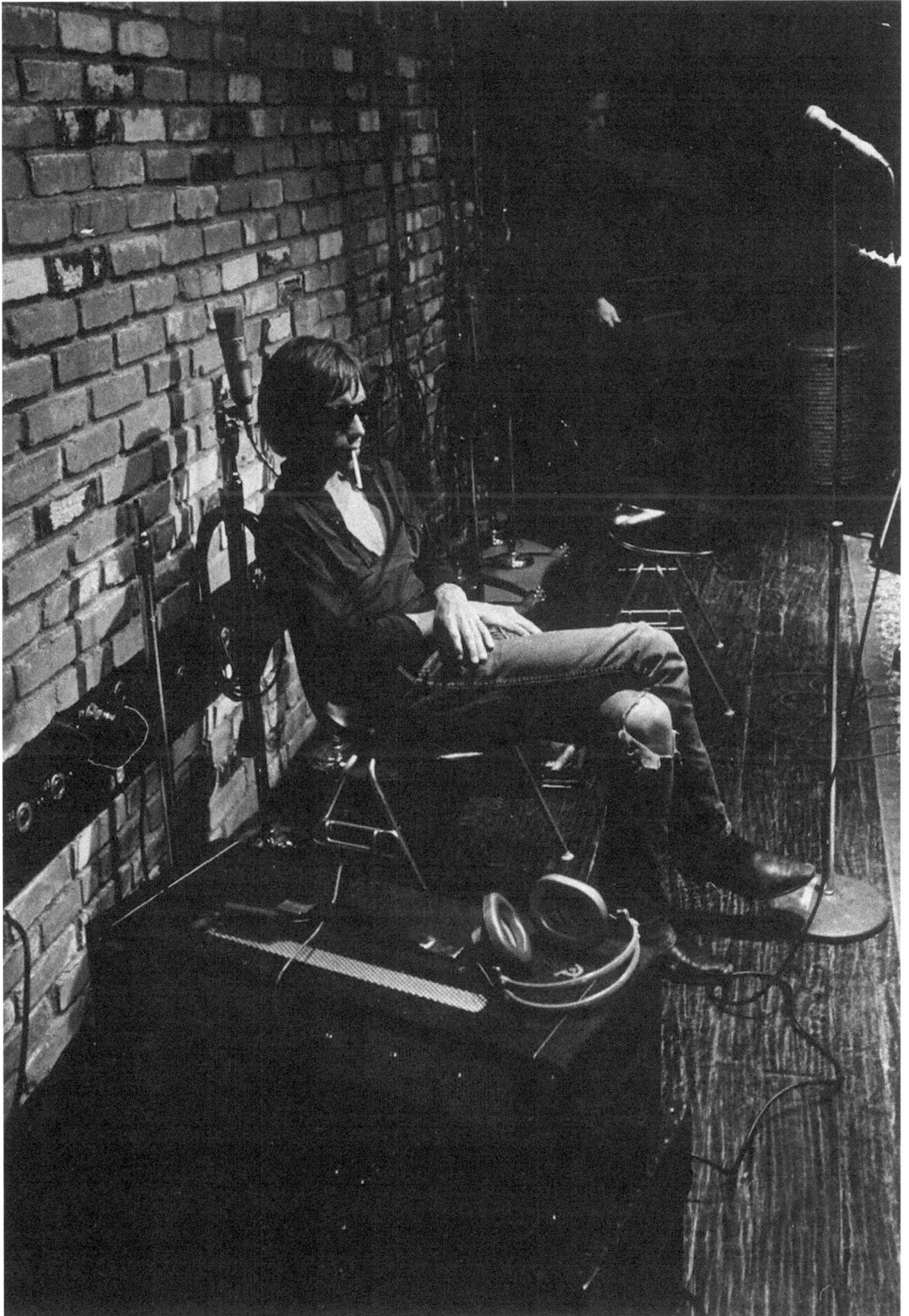

you include all of the "unofficial" sundry live recordings which still continue to flood the marketplace and in most cases only serve to dilute the Pop brand even further. Iggy also embarked on countless tours with an ever-rotating cast of backup musicians plucked from the ruins of bands which were first formed in The Stooges' wake. Blondie, Patti Smith Group, Sex Pistols, Damned. No matter where these Igg acolytes came from, he tapped them all for solo support.

Snap. What about James? Iggy also tapped Williamson but, after producing *New Values* (accredited) and *Soldier* (uncredited), James decided to tap himself out of the music business altogether.

James: "Well, that's more than a two beer discussion but the abbreviated version is that too many things were going wrong all at once and I needed to find a way to make my life more predictable. After I worked for a while in a few recording studios, I began having an interest in electronics. This was at the time when the PC was just emerging and I became fascinated by it. It was exciting in the way that rock 'n' roll had once been. Anyway, I worked very hard and managed to make a career out of it, but now I've come full circle and have rediscovered music as something I'm deeply interested in."

Snap. How about Ron? Never straying far from his hometown of Ann Arbor, Ron played with a number of bands including New Order, Destroy All Monsters, and New Race. In the meantime, Scott joined Sonic's Rendezvous Band, which had been started by Fred "Sonic" Smith of the MC5 a few years after the 5 fell apart in a manner not at all unlike what had befallen The Stooges. And as might be expected, both brothers' paths would cross every so often when Ron's DAM shared the bill with Scott's SRB.

Things got even tighter when Iggy decided to take three-fourths of SRB on a European tour with him, joined by Scott Thurston who had rejoined Team Pop a year earlier. Iggy even offered to keep SRB on for the recording of what would be his fourth solo record. But with Bowie back sniffing around for more, Scottie decided to head home instead, rather than run off to Berlin with them at the tour's end. "You had your chance!" Iggy would taunt Scott for years afterwards, but Rock Action was only doing what a lot of Iggy's musicians did: quit of their own volition long before they ever got sacked. That's because the singer's solo behavior was never far removed from his Stoogian heyday—the only difference being that The Igg now had better handlers and better tour money as befitting someone who was currently being *fêted* as "The Godfather Of Punk" at the close of the '70s . . . and the '80s . . . and the '90s . . .

And as each successive decade passed, the disbarred lay down the law firm of Asheton, Asheton, and Pop continued to do their own independent thing in their own independent time. But as good as some of that music was, there's no denying that what all three did separately never came even remotely close to what all three had done collectively as The Stooges. Which makes them, you know, just like The Beatles.

*** *** ***

In 1996, Iggy Pop was finally given the opportunity to go back into the studio and once and for all properly remix the alleged audio abomination both revered and reviled as *Raw Power*. He needn't have bothered— and this time we're not kidding, folks: he *really* needn't have bothered. Recently unsealed Grand Jury testimony from the global class action lawsuit THE PEOPLE VS. POP is telling. Here in his very own words, Dr. Frankenstooge finally admits that he meddled with things that man was meant to leave alone.

PROSECUTOR MORGAN: Look, I don't mind that your remix of *Raw Power* is the loudest album in history. As a matter of fact, speaking as a volume advocate from *way* back, I *applaud* you for mixing an album that's so loud you don't even have to turn your *amp* on to hear it.

DEFENDANT POP: [*laughs*]

PROSECUTOR MORGAN: But speaking on behalf of everyone who has that album memorized note for note, I *really* have a problem with how you faded down some of James Williamson's original guitar parts and faded up brand new ones, especially on "Your Pretty Face Is Going To Hell."

DEFENDANT POP: [*laughing*] I couldn't agree with you more!

PROSECUTOR MORGAN: Then why did you *do* it, sir?

DEFENDANT POP: Well, I had . . . you know . . . [*laughs*] It *seemed* like a good idea . . . I kinda did it on steroids. Well, a lot of people *did* complain about the *sound* of the original *Raw*—

PROSECUTOR MORGAN: Not anymore!

DEFENDANT POP: So now they love it.

PROSECUTOR MORGAN: After they heard *yours*? "You don't know what you've got 'till it's gone." People *really* like that original mix now.

DEFENDANT POP: Well, there ya go. So that's *great*. So whatever happens next, who knows? [*laughing*]

Maybe I'll let *Williamson* try one, *I* don't know.

The prosecution rests.

When Iggy's new version of *Raw Power* hit the racks a year later—some thirty years after the original Stooge-influenced punk revolution—yet *another* new generation of Stooge-infused fans were now fronting bands of their own. One of them, bassist Mike Watt, had been playing entire *sets* of Stooges covers in bands like Hellride and the Wylde Rattz. And because Watt had first met Ron Asheton when the Field Marshall came to one of Watt's gigs at St. Andrew's Hall in Detroit in the late '80s, it was perhaps inevitable that he and Ronnie would team up to record a new recording of "T.V. Eye" for the homo-neurotic glam flick *Velvet Goldmine*. That session went so well that they went on to write and record six new songs together with Ronnie singing two of them: "Screwing Around" and "Hot Shot." Not content with that, they then proceeded to entangle the entire area by cutting the air with a twelve minute rendition of "Fun House" replete with Watt on vocals and special guest Steve Mackay saxin' things up from behind.

By February 2001, Watt had taken up with Dinosaur Jr. member J Mascis and was playing in another band called The Fog. When they were about to play at the Blind Pig in Ann Arbor, J encouraged Watt to call Ronnie, who came down and jammed with them on a few Stooges songs. A month later, Ron joined them again at SXSW for a set that had grown to include the last nine songs from The Stooges' canon. That led to an additional fifteen gigs, including San Francisco, where Mackay once again showed up to blow out.

Watt: "The Stooges for the L.A. punk scene . . . we were all spread out from all these towns all over, but we'd all meet in Hollywood . . . we'd see the other hundred nuts, all these bands, the one thing we had in common was The Stooges. This band was so key for our scene, for our little universe, I can't speak for the whole world, but our scene . . . this band was it and Ronnie's the man. People would dislike you for liking them when we were growing up . . . but he's the man, very eloquent, great storyteller. He never tired of it, he'd tell me all these Stooges stories . . . but that first time was really wild."

And you thought *Iggy* was hard to understand.

Once again going forward to the past, Thurston Moore, who is ramrodding the first All Tomorrow's Parties event in Los Angeles, asks Watt to get Scottie to play with them. He does, and they call this new aggregation Asheton, Asheton, Mascis, and Watt. But this time when they take the stage on the Ides Of March, they have a number of guest singers joining in on the Stoogetivities: Pearl Jam's Eddie Vedder has no fun; Sonic Youth's Kim Gordon wants to be your dog, Stone Age Queen Josh Homme goes back to 1969, and Thurston has a real cool time. Later that August, AAMW get their second gig at the Pukkelpop Festival in Belgium before playing another four gigs in Europe.

Meanwhile, back in the States, the original puck of Pop is busy lining up hired guns for his next solo album when he starts to hear stories about how these brazen upstarts are ransacking stages across Europe and playing . . . playing *entire sets* of Stooges songs! To *tens of thousands* of Stooges fans! Like . . . like they were some kind of Stooges *tribute* band! Except they actually *are* Stooges!

And then a thought slowly dawns on The Iggmeister that maybe all of those songs from *The Stooges* and *Fun House* which have been faithfully covered over the decades are coalescing to send a solid message that's callin' out around the world: "Are you ready for an old school beat? We're still here so the time is right to get down on the street." Maybe. Just maybe. So The Igg cracks his Rolodex open to the letter A and makes a crucial phone call which will have serious rock 'n' roll ramifications for many years to come. The number to the house on Highlake has remained the same over the years and when the call goes through, Iggy has a pleasant conversation catching up on things with mother Ann. Then he asks her if she'd be kind enough to have Ronnie ring up Pop Manor in Miami when he gets home.

By December it's official: after a decades-long absence, the Ashetons will be reuniting with Iggy Pop to play on a couple of tracks off The Igg's upcoming album—a record that was corporately conceptualized to feature collaborations with some of the day's trendiest stars from Sum 41 to Green Day. Rock critics didn't like this at all, rightly seeing it as a desperate last-ditch attempt by the singer to tread water while trying to appear relevant. Because as everyone knows, namby-pamby duets and cheesy team-ups are the terminal symptoms of someone who's too old to cut the mustard on their own anymore. Besides, why would the great Iggy Pop enlist a bunch of Stage Door Stooges to back up his brag when he could have just as easily gone out and recorded an entire album with the equally great Ashetons? After all, didn't Iggy himself say in countless interviews on countless occasions that the best band he could ever possibly play with were The

Stooges? By the way, that's a rhetorical question 'cause the answer is: Yer darn tootin' he did. But we're getting ahead of ourselves again.

*** *** ***

The Ashetons hit Miami in mid January with a plan to write and record only two songs together with Iggy, but a funny thing happened on the way to the quorum. Once all the initial ". . . what took you so long . . ." catching up chit chat had been dispensed with and the serious task of making music began, a long dormant group chemistry rudely awoke from its restless slumber and promptly took over the sessions with the end result being that four new Stoogesongs had been created—the first since the '70s and 100% proof positive that not only were the Asheton brothers far from pasture material, but that they were the combustive catalyst that Iggy Pop needed to kick his karma back into high gear.

After the *Skull Ring* sessions had been completed, the inevitable rumors started circulating about a possible full-blown Stooges reunion. Ronnie was even talking about them perhaps doing a few sessions at Sun Studios in Memphis. The album hadn't even been mixed and in the hands of the record label yet when the first call came in: The Stooges had been offered a gig at Southern California's Coachella Festival outside of Palm Springs—*if* they'd reunite. So after Iggy decided that the time *was* right to get down on the street again, all that remained was finding a bass player who could do the deed and, more importantly, knew all the songs off by heart. Good thing you paid your dues playing all those Stooges covers, huh Mike?

Watt: "Yeah, Iggy tells me that 'Ronnie says you're the man' and I'm, like, 'fuck!' Then he talked to me for a long time about 'please don't wear flannel' and I said 'what about Levi's and Converse' and he says 'that's strong.' One of the most amazing conversations of my life. The interesting thing about front men, they have a different view; they don't look at the machine the same way as us mechanics."

Fittingly, the Coachella gig began with a stern warning from Iggy when he intoned: "Now look out!" before the band blasted through a roof-raisin' rendition of "Loose," followed by "Down On The Street," "1969," "I Wanna Be Your Dog," "T.V. Eye," "Dirt," "Real Cool Time," "No Fun," and "1970" before finally shutting things down with a soul-searing "Fun House."

And for anybody who might have straggled in late and weren't quite sure who they were watching, the master of ceremonies was kind enough to periodically remind them in no uncertain terms by proudly proclaiming: "We are The Stooges!" over and over and over again as if the singer himself couldn't believe his good fortune to be standing up there once again where he belonged with those he belonged with. Always decades ahead of their time, it literally *took* decades before the world finally caught up with The Stooges and was ready to acquiesce and accord them the veneration that they'd always richly deserved but had always been bitterly denied.

*** *** ***

There were no other plans for The Stooges at this point but the buzz was still on for the Stoogified *Skull Ring* which wouldn't come out until the fall. And although there were still a whole slew of solo promotions to complete, most notably a few gigs and a video with Sum 41, most everyone still had the talkin' Stooge blues—and *nobody* was willing to wait for the leaves to drop before they could see the Ashetons and Pop. So a few more Stoogeshows were slated, most notably a "homecoming of sorts" to be held on August 14th in Detroit.

But as hell bent as the band was about playing the Motor City again for their third reunited show, the "Luck Of The Stooges" stepped in once again as entire chunks of the Eastern power grid went down right before the show—or as noted Stoogecologist Brian J. Bowe would famously write later in his liner notes to the resultant *CREEM Presents The Stooges Live In Detroit* DVD: "*Raw* power? How about *no*

power?" And although the official Government explanation would have you believe otherwise, now the truth can finally be told about what *really* happened that night. For just as many have long suspected, the power went down a mere 0.554 milliseconds after Ron Asheton hit a particularly potent power chord during the sound check. When it was mentioned to Ronnie that it was *he* who had killed the juice to the optimistically named DTE Energy Music Center, The Stooges' Field Marshall adjusted his aviators and smiled, preferring to let the music do the talking.

Once the DTE's entire electrical system had been replaced, the show was rescheduled for eleven days later and The Stooges did not disappoint the overflow crowd. This was their longest set yet with the addition of "Skull Ring," "Not Right," "Little Doll," and a reprise of "I Wanna Be Your Dog," all with Mackay saxiting, stage left.

The Stooges' long-awaited new studio album, *The Weirdness*, came out in March 2007 and with that they became the darlings of SXSW: interviews, panels, record store signings, and even a gig at Stubbs BBQ ensured that once again they were the hottest ticket in town. As a sign of how uncannily tight the band had become, when Watt's bass died during "Skull Ring," the old bass player in Ronnie caught the sudden lack of bottom and, without missing a beat, he immediately picked up the slack until a replacement switch could be made. In fact, so seamless was Ron's transition that a few amateur ink-stained wretches even went so far as to claim that The Stooges were playing to a canned backing tape! Which, of course, is complete and utter nonsense. They've never used a tape during any of their live performances and they never will—which explains yet *another* unsolved mystery: why The Stooges have never been invited to play at a Presidential inauguration.

*** *** ***

These lip-synchin' Stooges then embarked on a twelve city American tour, their first properly done jaunt of the States in that this time there'd be no more riding in the back of a van and *definitely* no more low-bridging the equipment truck while driving to the next gig—right, Rock? It's at this point in the proceedings that you might want to get out a wall map of the USA and a handful of push-pins to chart their progress as they went from station to station. The only thing missing was Conductor James calling out each stop along the route as The Stooges started off in Washington, D.C. and then proceeded through a "Night Train" litany to Boston! New York City! Philly! Detroit! Chicago! Denver! Frisco! L.A.! Seattle! before

finally ending up getting their shoes shined on Beale Street in Memphis.

On second thought, maybe you'd better unfold a giant Rand McNally World Atlas instead so's you can follow the Detroit Globetrotters as they further flexed their Motor City muscle all over Planet Stooge. Because since that first one-off big pay check gig at Coachella in 2003, the hardest working reunited band in show business proceeded to get up offa that thing and play close to two hundred concerts. Got your push-pins ready? Then all aboard . . . the Stooge Train! The US of A! United Kingdom! Ireland! Canada! France! Spain! Germany! Austria! Denmark! Poland! Israel! Norway! Sweden! Finland! Belgium! Greece! Croatia! Russia! Macedonia! Netherlands! Iceland! Portugal! Hungary! Serbia! Slovakia! Slovenia! Italy! Turkey! Japan! Mexico! Argentina! Brazil! Australia! New Zealand! And we aren't just talkin' about a few measly one-offs here because many of these countries requested—nay, *demanded*—that return visits be made to accommodate the massive overflow of crowds that swarmed to each performance.

And to show that even The Luck Of The Stooges had a good sense of humor, the very last gig of 2008—one which was to have been played in Sarajevo, Herzegovina on October 1st—had to be cancelled by the state government. As a result of severe protest rioting demanding the cancellation of an upcoming queer festival, the ruling regime was concerned for *The Stooges*' safety if they showed up. Which reminds us of a story that Mr. Matheu likes to tell . . .

Robert: "One night when the reconstituted Stooges were playing All Tomorrow's Parties at the Queen Mary in Long Beach, James Williamson and Scott Thurston came to the show and made their way backstage. When they both walked into the double-wide dressing room, The Igg's long-suffering manager Art Collins and I left to give everyone some private space. As we walked towards the stage, Art suddenly turned to me and said: 'Hey, that's the *Metallic K.O.* Stooges in that room! Maybe we should open the door and throw some bottles!' "

Yeah, right. As if The Stooges would ever again have to suffer the eggs and ice cubes of misguided fortune. And speaking of fortunes, do you remember that "last ever" Stooges show back in 1974? You know, the one in which Iggy valiantly weathers a brutal onslaught of audience brutality only to bravely blast back: "You're payin' five bucks and I'm makin' ten thousand, baby! *So screw ya!*" Sure you do.

Well, Iggy may have slightly exaggerated his remuneration for dramatic effect that night, but these

days The Stooges have definitely had the last laugh on every single no-nothing loser who ever cast aspirations on their art and had them pegged as penny ante pikers and perennial losers. Ten thousand, baby? The Stooges earned a whopping *twenty million dollars* in the past five years. Now *there's* a career turnaround if ever there *was* one.

*** *** ***

In 1973, Harvey Kurtzman—who had created MAD magazine for Bill Gaines' EC Comics in the '50s and then created *Little Annie Fanny* for Hugh Hefner's *Playboy* magazine in the '60s—went with Monty Python member and film director Terry Gilliam to see The Stooges as part of the research he was doing for a *Little Annie Fanny* episode on glitter rock.

"Iggy Pop came out and he did a couple of songs," Kurtzman later recalled to fellow artist John Holmstrom in PUNK magazine. "He did one song where the verse was one word repeated over and over again: *Motherfucker.* But he had *style.* He had *substance.* He had an unusual technique that was nimble talent."

But it wasn't just Iggy: *every single member of The*

Stooges had that same nimble talent. How else to explain their agile ability to collectively dodge all manner of projectiles in public and withstand all manner of defeat in private? How else to explain the sheer enormity of will power it took for them to play their music in the face of seemingly insurmountable odds? Because no other band in the history of rock 'n' roll *ever* suffered through such cascades of relentless physical and mental abuse. Their records didn't sell. Their shows often ended with an abrupt spasm of violence. And when they finally *did* fade away, no one even thought enough of them to call for their return—least of all The Stooges themselves.

So say a prayer for those valued band members who are unable to join us for this well deserved commemoration of durability—and raise a full glass to those who, thankfully, still are. But whatever you do, don't you *dare* dishonor *any* of them by doing them the disservice of thinking that this book somehow heralds the end of an era. Because it doesn't. To paraphrase the great Carl Sandburg:

The Stooges, yes.

The Stooges will live on.

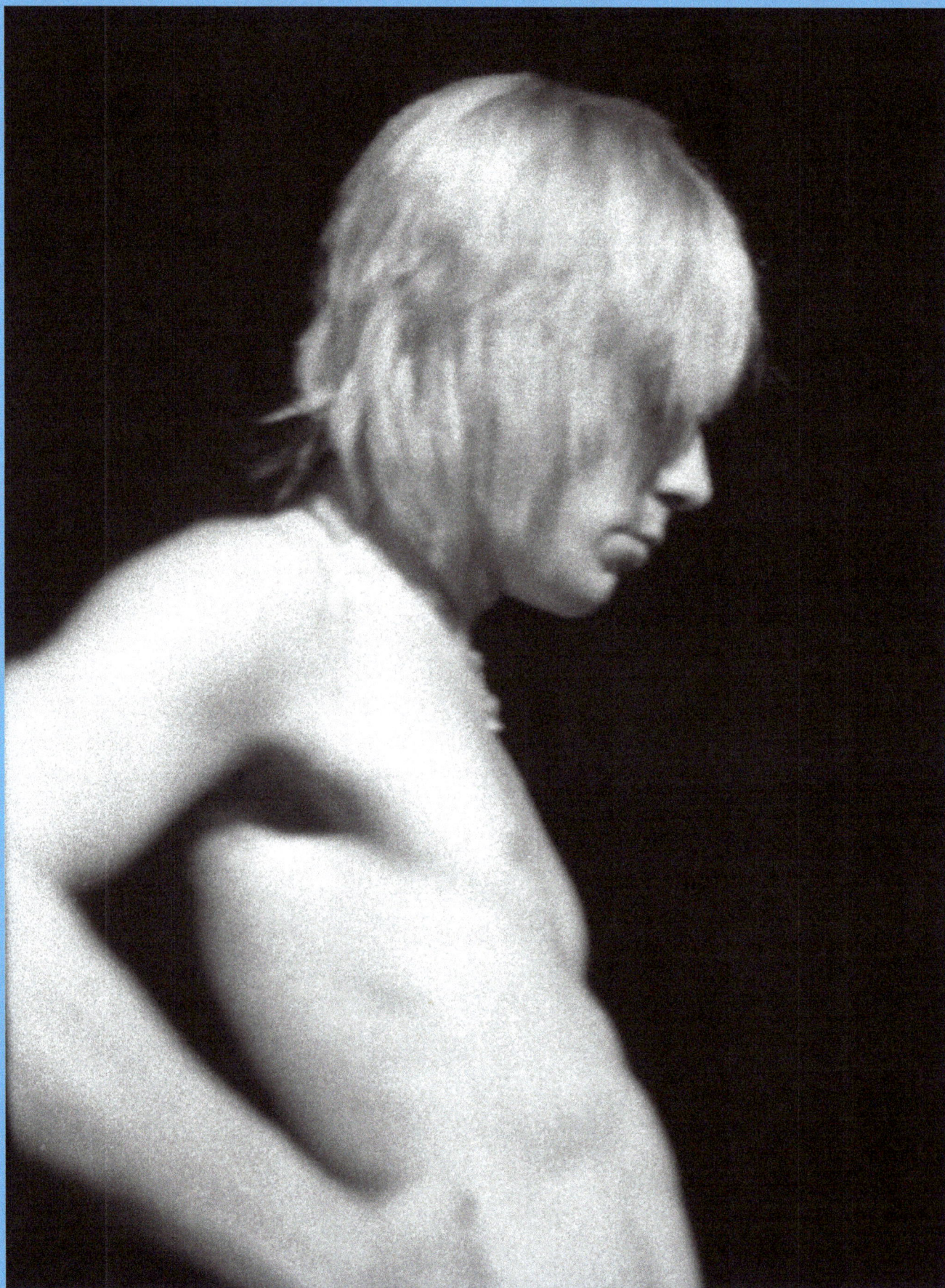

**photographed by
John Catto**

The Victory Burlesque Theatre,
Toronto. January 25th 1974.

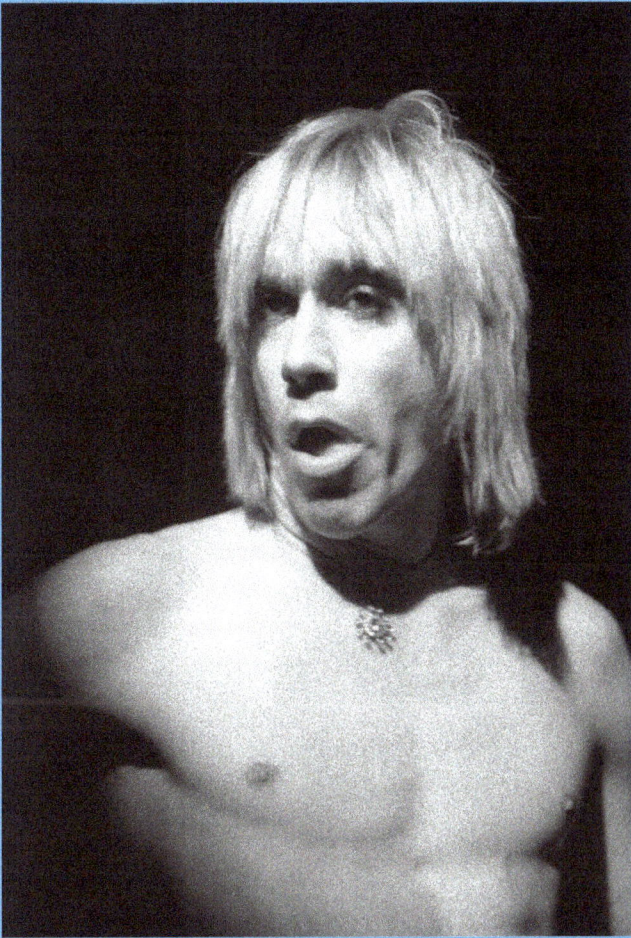

photographed by
Robert Sikora

The Victory Burlesque Theatre,
Toronto. January 25th 1974.

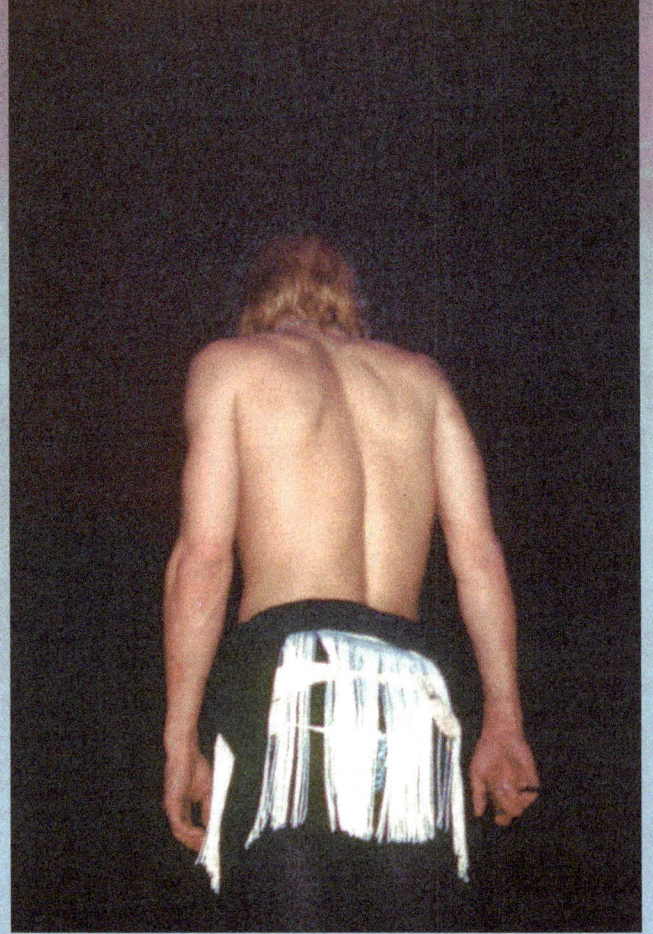

THE ALBUMS REVIEWED
THE STOOGES
by **Dave DiMartino**

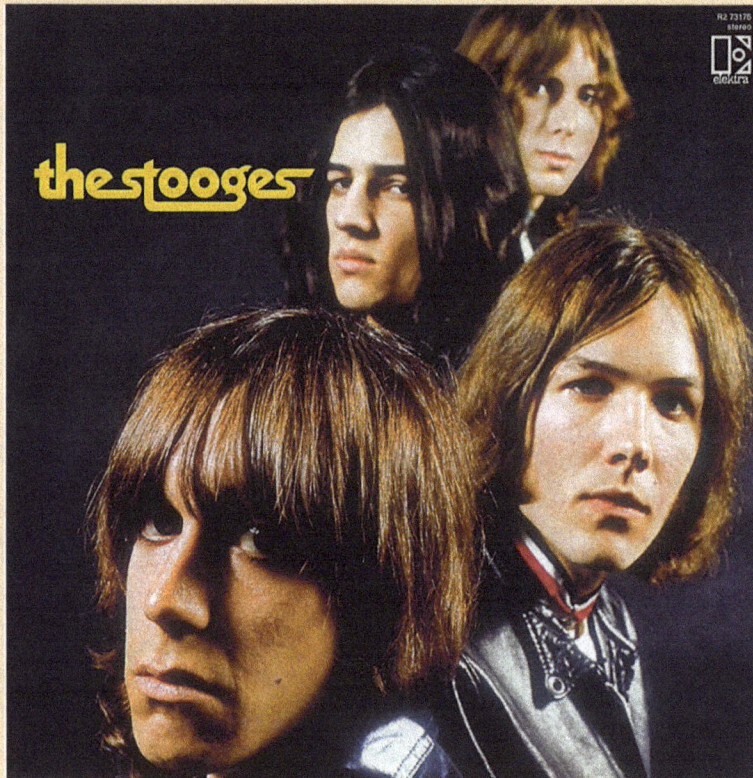

"There must be not more than a hundred words on that album," Iggy Pop has said of The Stooges' debut. "So I made each one count."

And so it is that today, a full forty years after *The Stooges* was made, those who were too young to have heard this classic album at the time it was released—too young to fully grasp the irony of it being released the same week that Janis Joplin, the Jefferson Airplane, and Crosby, Stills & Nash were to perform onstage at the cultural milestone that was the Woodstock festival—can hear it with 21st Century ears, removed from any context but today's. They can hear it for what it is, rather than what it isn't. And if they do, they'll hear exactly what Iggy meant.

There is not a note of fat on this album. There are no wasted words. Even today, when I play it, I continue to marvel at the precision not only of the words that Iggy Pop sings, but of the actual syllables. Consider these eight words: Another, Favorite, Somebody, Telephone,

Cigarette, Prettiest, Happiness, Everything. They are, in order of occurrence, the only words with more than two syllables on this entire album. And I'm not going to count, but trust me here: the vast majority of the remaining lyrics have only one syllable.

Maybe in 1969 songs with such titles as "Real Cool Time" seemed the height of doltdom: a deliberate, irony-filled lunge for being aggressively stupid. But hearing it today? No way. Ron Asheton's guitar wash, Dave Alexander's wandering bass, and Scott Asheton's simple but accurate drum pounding no longer sound amateurish compared to the instrumental dexterity displayed by contemporaries such as Jimi Hendrix, up there on the Woodstock stage: they sound like a basic stylistic prototype that would influence several generations of musicians to come. Which they most certainly did. More fascinating, at least to me, is how Iggy's sparse lyrics now seem so obviously like the polished jewels they were:

Can I come over tonight?
Can I come over tonight?
What do you think I wanna do?
That's right.
Can I come over tonight?

Is there any doubt whatsoever what is being sung here?

Having heard this album when it emerged in 1969, I have to confess to still hearing it for what it isn't. But what's interesting to me today is: what it isn't has changed. In the years that would follow this album's release, scattered artists would emerge—the Modern Lovers, the Ramones, the Sex Pistols—that would eventually be perceived as following in The Stooges' footsteps in some palpable way. This is the accepted wisdom, and if you'd asked me in my younger days to illustrate this with examples, I might have pointed out the obvious. I would have told you that the Sex Pistols covered "No Fun;" that Ramones tracks like "Beat On The Brat" and "Now I Wanna Sniff Some Glue" echoed both the boredom and absurdity of Iggy's singing "Now I'm gonna be twenty-two, I say oh my and a boo hoo" in "1969;" and the Modern Lovers' classic "She Cracked"—with its unforgettable passage: "She cracked. I won't. She did things that I don't. She'd eat garbage, eat shit, get stoned. I stay alone, eat health food at home"—was similar in its lyrical theme to The Stooges' "Not Right."

But here's the thing. I'm not so sure that's true now.

As the song's very title implies, it was 1969 when The Stooges made their grand entrance with this first album and Iggy declared: "There's nothing here for me and you. Another year with nothing to do." Several years would pass before the Pistols covered "No Fun," the Buzzcocks sang "Boredom," and the Clash confided they were so bored with the USA; several years would pass before the boredom The Stooges noted would become commoditized and utilized as, essentially, a musical movement's marketing tool. And try as they might, those bands did not sound like The Stooges. The Ramones? God love 'em, but their deliberately simplistic musical approach was accompanied by an undercurrent of irony, sly winks, and humor. Go back again and listen to this first Stooges album. Irony? Sly winks? If anything, there's an undercurrent of personal desperation on most of these tracks. Better yet, if you want to see what separates The Stooges from these other bands—especially the Modern Lovers, whom I particularly admire—check out Iggy's lyrics completely stripped from their musical context in "Not Right."

She
Not right
I want something
I want something
Tonight

I want something
I want something
Alright
But she
Can't help
'Cause she's not right

No, no, no, no

And it's always
And it's always this way

Forty years ago, if wanted poetry mixed with my music, I could always pull out *Strange Days* and hear that song about what happens when the still sea conspires an armor and her sullen and aborted currents breed tiny monsters. I'm not sure I would have played *The Stooges* for the same reason then, but I might now.

There are many reasons why my favorite Stooges album is their first, and John Cale's production is not a small one. For all the talk about the chaotic mess and musical amateurishness that represented The Stooges' early days, there is a very clean, stratified air to this recording that is almost the polar opposite of that found on Cale's earlier recording with the Velvet Underground, *White Light/White Heat*. "Sister Ray" and "I Heard Her Call My Name" had been a deliberately messy slab of noise in which the Velvets' instruments had blended into one pulsating monolith of sound. But on *The Stooges*, every player, every sound, and every lyric is clearly audible. Ron Asheton's guitar, whether chording or holding a sustain that never evaporates, is an object of beauty. There are no wasted notes, not a single one. Dave Alexander's bass—a tad more audible on the original mixes packaged with Rhino's 2005 reissue—is fascinatingly exploratory and by no means the solid rock around which the other musicians play. Scott Asheton's drumming, on the other hand, probably is, and it's simply perfect here. Mostly though, it is Iggy Pop's voice that is easiest to focus on here—and the words that he is singing.

Most interesting of all to me is this: *The Stooges* is a profoundly influential album. We all know that. But it does not sound like it was made in 1969. If it came out today—in a world without The Stooges—no one would raise an eyebrow and call it old-fashioned. But it doesn't sound like anything that would come out today. It really doesn't sound like anything else but the first Stooges album.

I can't think of another band in all of popular music that ever has managed to sound like The Stooges, and at this late date, I don't think any band ever will.

Iggy already used up the good words, for starters.

1970: THE COMPLETE FUN HOUSE SESSIONS

Be seated.

Now, I want you to remember that upon first being confronted with this massive monument, my initial gut reaction was to take the easy way out by irresponsibly spewing forth an unsubstantiated litany of absurd analogies instead of prudently sticking to the facts and keeping things in their proper level-headed perspective. In fact, I was even going to go so far as to proclaim that, insofar as genuine Edward R. Murrow *Hear It Now* moments go, these recordings capture a rare moment in time that's easily the historical equivalent of being a disciple present at the Last Supper.

But then I thought about it and realized that such an outrageous claim would be an out 'n' out blasphemous lie because *1970: The Complete Fun House Sessions* is far and away the better bargain of the two. After all, at a whopping eight hours in length, not only are these seminal sessions in all likelihood a

whole lot longer in duration than that classic bread-breaking meal, there's the added bonus attraction of not having to suffer through any foreign language barrier while you're busy chowing down.

That's assuming, of course, that you happen to be thoroughly fluent in Mister Pop's patented brand of Stoogespeak. If you're not, however, then dare to beware because these seven discs are a harrowing excursion into a swirling abyss where even the strongest of men get sucked in and shrunken into simpering weak-kneed boys; to underestimate the unrelenting, unbridled force of this daunting document is to do so at your own risk—and I do mean *daunting*. No doubt many a raw recruit will blanch at the prospect of having to endure a basic training routine that includes having to wade waist deep through no less than thirty different versions of "Loose." But if you think you're fan enough to handle not only that but a whole lot more, then grab your allotted ration of peanut butter and slide inside.

Stoogeologists have long debated the relative merits of *Fun House*'s finely-honed savagery vis-à-vis *Raw Power*'s seedy brutality for well over a quarter century now, but in all that time they've never had access to such exhaustive aural evidence as is presented here. Now such discussions can be seen in a startling new light as The Stooges' studio methodology is finally revealed in enlightening detail for the very first time.

And what a story these tapes tell. Anyone expecting to plunge into a goldbricking *Metallic K.O.* sideshow of dissipated decay is going to be sorely disappointed because *1970: The Complete Fun House Sessions* confirms what many a staunch Stooge supporter has always maintained: that not only were The Stooges a most *powerful* band, they were a most *professional* one as well. Not since the release of *The Complete Charlie Parker On Verve* has there been such a unique opportunity to candidly observe the meticulous methodology of a major recording artist in a recording studio for such an extended length of time. Granted, not once on that ten disc box set does Parker ever pause to inquire: "Is there a beer in there? Can I have a sip?" as everybody's favorite well-mannered boy does before a particularly heated run-through of "1970." But such extraneous studio talk is kept to a minimum as the group gets down to the serious business of recording their second album in a no-nonsense, workman-like fashion that may surprise some.

And ramrodding this aural attack is none other than Sgt. Stooge himself: a disciplined, no nonsense bandleader who relentlessly whips the group into shape as if he were Jack Webb playing Marine Corps drill instructor Jim Moore in *The D.I.* "Hold it a second, just a second," Iggy says, interrupting a take of "Down On The Street" to address Dave Alexander. "Listen, there's an extra . . . could one of your strings be ringing that you're not playing? Could that be possible? I hear a huge bass ring going through. Let's try it again."

Since most of the songs on *1970: The Complete Fun House Sessions* are recorded live in the studio literally dozens of times, of particular interest to literature lovers everywhere is the way in which Iggy's famous stream of consciousness lyrics evolve as the sessions proceed. Always known for his ability to improvise from scratch, Iggy's *Fun House* lyrics swagger into the studio as partially-formed nebulous templates which are slack enough to allow him the luxury of liberally changing the content and rhymes of each song from take to take. Hearing Iggy sing: "Well, I'm flying on a red hot weenie! Yeah, I'm riding on a big hot dog!" during a version of "Loose" is easily well worth the five hundred bucks you'll have to shell out on the black market to hear such alternative pearls of Poppian prose.

And make no mistake: you *will* dig deep and cough up that cool half a grand because this bludgeoning behemoth only exists in a paltry limited edition of 3,000 numbered copies, all of which have long since been scooped up. Sure, you *could* muster out and order the severely scaled-back, two disc civilian side platter like some kind of rank amateur, but you can bet your furlough pass that a *professional* connoisseur of cacophony wouldn't settle for anything less than the full seven course feast which culminates with the band serving up their mess hall *Stooge de résistance*: an ungarnished eighteen minute version of "L.A. Blues" that'll leave you sonically sated and crawlin' from the *Fun House*.

Alright now you sons of Stooges, you know how I feel. Oh, and I will be proud to play this wonderful record for you guys anytime, anywhere.

That's all.

THE ALBUMS REVIEWED

RAW POWER

by **Ivan Suvanjieff**

Vindicated prophets are not happy people.
— Andrei Codrescu

Fuck you all. I was right.

Legions revere Iggy And The Stooges, but it wasn't always this way. For those of us who were true fans back in the day, the gala history rewrite continues to not only annoy, but actually astound. People I know who never once put on a Stooges album in my presence are now telling me how great they were, and are. This is called "hindsight" cos that's what it is when you pull your pointed head outta your pretentious ass.

If you were in high school in the metro Detroit area in the early 1970s and were at all interested in rock 'n' roll, you had to work pretty hard to avoid seeing Iggy And The Stooges. They played all the time at high schools, ice rinks, concert halls, and more. And The Stooges, as you've heard, were once considered a joke. "Can't play their instruments," was a common charge. "The singer is just a weirdo," was regular flatulence. I remember hearing all the stories about The Stooges from older kids in the late '60s. The stories of the band having stage props including

toilets, vacuum cleaners, you name it, were numerous and free-flowing. The same people who told me how totally inept the band was kept filling me in week after week as to the latest Stooges craziness. Everybody loves a train wreck as long as they're not on the tracks, right?

Raw Power was released in early 1973 and if you take a quick look at the hits of that year . . .

01. Tie A Yellow Ribbon Round The Ole Oak Tree » Tony Orlando & Dawn
02. Bad Bad Leroy Brown » Jim Croce
03. Killing Me Softly With His Song » Roberta Flack
04. Let's Get It On » Marvin Gaye
05. My Love » Paul McCartney & Wings
06. Why Me » Kris Kristofferson
07. Crocodile Rock » Elton John
08. Will It Go Round In Circles » Billy Preston
09. You're So Vain » Carly Simon
10. Touch Me In The Morning » Diana Ross

. . . you grock that The Stooges were not dancing to the beat of the day or the era, they were dancing to the beat of the living dead. For me and my high school crew, *Raw Power* represented the howl of misunderstood and somewhat deserved pain; the cry of hopeless battle.

At the average high school Friday night house party you'd regularly hear J. Geils, Elton John, and the aforementioned Top 10 radio swill—that is, until we arrived. We always took our favorite albums to parties and *Raw Power* was there at the top of the stack, which also included Bowie, Lou Reed, and Roxy Music. We would wait until everyone was fairly loaded and then we'd put *Raw Power* on. I'm thankful that *Raw Power* hit the cut-out bins almost immediately after its release. It only cost a dollar back then and, having had a number of copies of this culturally gargantuan album broken over my head by angry jocks, I appreciated the deep discount.

How could a bunch of teenagers *not* love "Search And Destroy"? Drop the needle in the groove and the first words out of Iggy's mouth are: "I'm a street-walkin' cheetah with a heart full of napalm. I'm a runaway son of the nuclear A-bomb." Which neatly summed up my feelings in a couplet. And the sound of Williamson's guitar was that of our twisted teen souls: the howl of the horny and stoned; the poetry of the possessed dispossessed. Whether the band wanted to, or realized it or not, *Raw Power* was a major hosing of all imbued with lovey dovey peacey groovy. Finding no way to traverse workaday 1973, The Stooges were forging a perverted musical geography for the next savage state. Around the same time that The Stooges took the stage in their triumphant homecoming Detroit gig at Ford Auditorium that March, Henry Kissinger and Le Duc Tho could not agree on the shape of the table at the Paris peace talks—and *they* won a Nobel Peace Prize! The Stooges? Not so much.

In 1973, when you went to shop for stereo equipment, the salesman would put on Steely Dan or some other "accomplished" music to prove the mettle of their product. I wasn't fully appreciated for insisting on playing the entire *Raw Power* album at full volume on the Marantz 6300 direct drive turntable I eventually bought and still use.

Listening to *Raw Power* today, it's hard not to marvel at its darkness and its challenge to the listener. Iggy was at his height of poetic power, poisoned as it was. *Raw Power* held a mirror up to our dirty Detroit faces and we shouted along as Iggy spit: "Honey, come and be my enemy so I can love you true."

Ron Asheton was a friend of mine. My groups the Ramrods and the 27 played with Destroy All Monitors, which is what we called the Monsters. Ron was also a raconteur nonpareil. I used to sit transfixed as Ron would roll out story after story so many times over the years. We all miss him—and that makes a

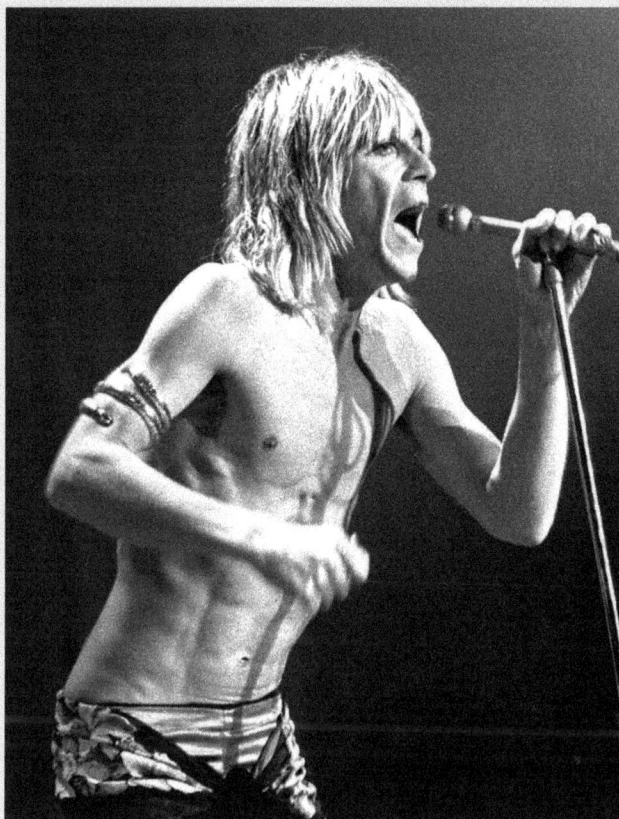

remembrance of the third Stooges studio LP awkward. The decision to bring James Willamson into the band changed things, to say the least. Old-school Stooges fan only seem to begrudgingly like *Raw Power*. Well, they're Ron's fans who resent that Williamson took over on guitar and leaving Ron "demoted" to bass. Or so the story goes. But did Ron not play bass in James' band the Chosen Few? Which leads to the idea that it was this new guitarist who doused the bonfire of Iggy's drug use with napalm. But what . . . Williamson was just some unknown entity? His presence disrupted The Stooges' church-based sewing circle? As the saying goes: "I only introduced you to her. I didn't put a gun to your head and make you marry her."

I was right about *Raw Power* from the very beginning and fuck you very much I enjoy being right. It was a colossus when it was released in 1973 and it's only grown in stature and legend as the decades drag on. The list of acts who now champion *Raw Power* and The Stooges in general is endless—and most of these acts blow dogs. Yet I'm angry because for over 35 years I've known that *Raw Power* is a quintessential, thoroughly tortured masterpiece. And I've said just that aloud as often as possible. You weren't having any of it though, were ya?

Someone once said that: "Art is what you reject." Well, *Raw Power* is true, high art. It was rejected, it was humiliated, it was scorned. If The Stooges were painters, then *Raw Power* would be their *Guernica*. And here it is now in your fat stupid face, essential and eternal.

THE ALBUMS REVIEWED
METALLIC K.O.
by **Brian J. Bowe**

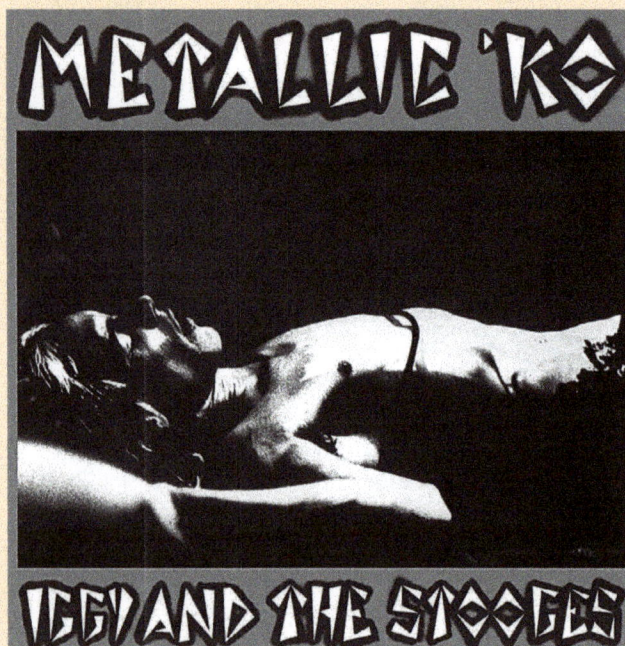

Since its release in 1976, The Stooges' Metallic K.O. has been wrapped in mystery and legend. This live document of the band's final implosion is an imperfect recording of outright hostility between performer and audience. It is so easy to focus on its outrageousness that it would be simple to dismiss it as a novelty record—some sort of protopunk Blowfly with an attitude.

Focusing on the album's outlandishness does it a great disservice because *Metallic K.O.* is so much more than dick jokes and smashed bottles. It is, in fact, the perfect artistic representation of madness, self-loathing, and psychic terror. In it, everybody's favorite well-mannered boy Iggy Pop spills out the contents of his ransacked psyche, and it is not a pretty sight. All the while, the rest of the band holds on tight with both hands while taking the music farther and farther out in brutal reaction to Iggy's disintegration.

Metallic K.O. has given Iggy a case of the heebie jeebies for years—and it's easy to see why. It's an uncomfortable album, somewhere between a car wreck and a snuff film. However, one of the recurring threads throughout The Stooges' *oeuvre* is that they always functioned like the antenna of society, capturing the psycho-emotional content of the moment. From the youthful boredom of *The Stooges* to the high-wattage experimentation of *Fun House* to the searing

explosiveness of *Raw Power*, the band always *sounded like* how they *felt*. So, judging from the sounds on *Metallic K.O.*, The Stooges at the end felt like a million dreams shattering in hostility, self-hatred, and drug-fueled delusion. In other words, they felt like shit.

Metallic K.O. is often believed to be a document of a single concert, but in reality it was recorded over two separate nights: October 6th, 1973 and February 9th, 1974, both at a theater in Detroit called the Michigan Palace. (Movie buffs and hip-hop fans will recognize that location from the Eminem movie *8 Mile*, but in real life the ornate former theater is now a parking garage.) Both shows have subsequently been released in their entirety on a set called *Metallic 2X K.O.*

By 1973, The Stooges were heading nowhere good. *Raw Power* was released in the spring of that year with great hopes that The Stooges would ride the David Bowie/MainMan glam train to new heights of fabulousness. The Stooges played one show of the *Raw Power* material at Detroit's Ford Auditorium in March 1973 before the deal with MainMan fell apart. "After that," Iggy told me in 2005, "any other live shows that you come across, you're hearing a band left to its own devices."

Such was the *Raw Power* lineup of Iggy, James Williamson on guitar, Ron Asheton on bass, and Scott Asheton on drums, augmented by future Heartbreaker Scott Thurston (that's Tom Petty Heartbreaker, not Johnny Thunders Heartbreaker). Not only were The Stooges suffering from a bad management deal, they were also the victims of public indifference. "We were serious about everything," said Scott Asheton. "But it got to a point where there was nothing to be serious about because nobody wanted us."

With the band left to try and conquer the world on its own, Iggy's performances began turning more tortured and weird. Lacking the good sense to just go away, The Stooges spent 1973 embarking on strange little tours, including runs of shows at Max's Kansas City in New York and the Whisky A Go Go in Hollywood. Meanwhile, The Stooges had turned into a circus sideshow, with Iggy the primary head-chomping geek.

"It was pretty wild and wooly on the personal side. I'll leave that to your imagination," Iggy said. "On the musical side, we were still trying to forge ahead. In other words, we weren't standing still for all of the chitter-chatter about this band in that period. Listen, heroin wasn't chic yet unless you were the Rolling Stones. We were *baaaaad* fucking news and people were scared to admit they knew us."

Even the band members found Iggy's behavior strange and engaging. "For me, every show was like I was in the audience," Scott Asheton said. "I had no idea what he was going to do. I was as interested as the audience as far as what was going to happen next. For me, every show was kind of like *going* to a show. I had the best seat in the house. It made it more entertaining for me."

Iggy was doing battle with his stage persona, egged on (no pun intended) by people who would give him drugs and instigate his antisocial tendencies. "People want to give him stuff and they want to make him a little monster," Ron Asheton told me. "People were always shoving things in his face and into his hand. It's really hard being Iggy and it's even harder if you're expected to top yourself every night and you've got *two* shows every night." But, Ron added: "We were there to take him wherever he wanted to go."

So by the time The Stooges made it to the Michigan Palace, the weirdness had consumed Iggy and the rest of The Stooges were compelled to follow him. In the middle of Iggy's dissipated, decimated, and desiccated state, the band attacked the music with aplomb. They didn't so much exhibit the precision of a watchmaker; it was more like precision of a crack special forces unit: it wasn't always pretty, there was frequent collateral damage, but just making it to the end of the day alive was a victory.

Even as the prospects for The Stooges were dimming, the band was well-practiced and tight. Scott Thurston pounds the piano mercilessly, offering a vague reminder that this is supposed to be rock 'n' roll. There's something about Williamson's playing that is distinctly unfriendly, as though it carries with it the suggestion of great psychic discomfort. His approach is lethal. "James has a very intense Scorpionic energy," Iggy said. "James will just come in and basically run you through. That's the way he plays. It's not blunt. It's not a blunt instrument, there's an edge to it. But he's out to kill."

If Williamson added sharp lethality, the rhythm section added a certain musical panache—somehow the brothers Asheton possessed hearts big enough to create beauty in the midst of insanity. "Scott has a particular ear on drums and he plays the song. He doesn't just beat on the drums," Iggy said. "Take a look at Ron's hands sometime, which is what attracted me to him as a musician in the first place, because I was looking for people who could go somewhere beyond local bars and third bill at the ballrooms. Ron has a *fine arts* pair of hands and you hear a certain elegance to his touch and his playing."

There is a distinct difference between the two shows documented on *Metallic K.O.* In the October 1973

show, the band sounds a little crispy around the edges, but not totally fried. Iggy rails against the "buttfuckers trying to rule this world" in "Head On" and before "Open Up And Bleed" there's some audience abuse: "Who hates The Stooges?" asks Iggy, to some applause. "Well, we don't hate *you*, we don't even care." But there's also some standard rock-singer-to-audience banter and, in total, the show comes off more or less like a standard rock show, albeit a little bit bent.

The February 1974 show is way more *out there*. The original LP took "Rich Bitch," "Cock In My Pocket," and "Louie Louie" from that concert. The full show starts off with a brutal "Heavy Liquid" which is soon followed by a version of "I Got Nothing" (which Iggy introduces as "I Got Shit") that serves as a reminder of the cracked glam potential of The Stooges. Iggy's speech is slurred and he introduces songs with mock formality like some tweaked out Lawrence Welk: "For this evening's next selection, I would be proud to present a song that was co-written by my Mother entitled 'I Got My Cock In My Pocket.'" On "Rich Bitch" he taunts the crowd: "You're payin' five bucks and I'm makin' ten thousand, baby. *So screw ya!*"

Artistically, the highlight of the 1974 show is a tortured version of "Gimme Danger," which Iggy sings with extreme pathos. It's an intimate delivery, each line a window into Iggy's suffering. "I wanna be touched and I'm gonna be loved," he howls, "and I'm not afraid to say that I need you more than you need me." The wretchedness, self-hatred, and vulnerability he expresses is the same sentiment underpinning much of the best punk rock: souls damaged by modern society, reaching out, yet unable to connect, so lashing out is a way of self-preservation. Which Iggy does on the Welkian countdown to "Cock In My Pocket," when he yells: "A-one, two, *FUCK YOU, PRICKS!*"

Iggy heckles the audience, and they respond by hurling missiles—ice, eggs, bottles—which are audible on the recording. Finally, the act devolves into a profane rendition of "Louie Louie" that Iggy honed years earlier playing Ann Arbor frat parties. "I never thought it would come to this, baby," he says. In defeat, The Stooges planted the seeds for their own enduring legacy: The Stooges Are Dead! Long Live The Stooges! At the end of that final show, standing amidst the hurled debris from a bloodthirsty audience, Iggy says: "You nearly killed me, but you missed again so you have to keep trying next week."

"Next week" may have turned into three decades, but The Stooges *did* return, triumphant in their own strange way, with the knowledge that they were right to believe they were something special. And while *Metallic K.O.* spooked Iggy and marked the beginning of years in the wilderness, it electrified generations of listeners and assured them that it was OK to be messed-up, freaked-out, and fucked up. That it was OK for artists to put their most ugly emotions on public display. That it was OK to open up and bleed.

THE ALBUMS REVIEWED

KILL CITY

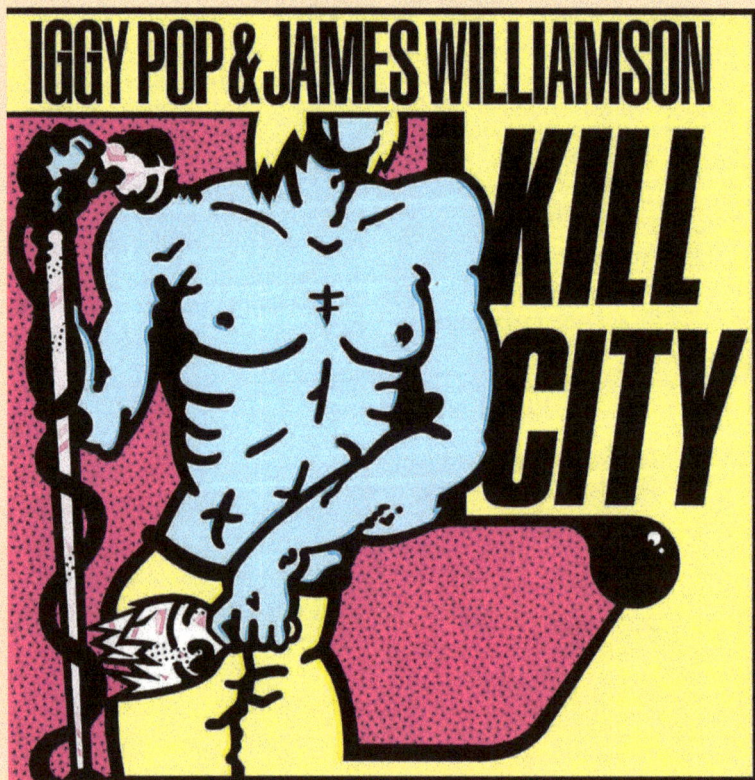

I bought this long-lost missing link between *Raw Power* **and** *The Idiot* **when it first came out some zillion years ago, at which point I lauded it as quite the auditory accomplishment. But that's** *nothing* **compared to how enthused I am about** *Kill City* **now that it's finally been remixed from the original masters under the watchful eye of album producer Strait James himself—even if he isn't actually credited as such on the record; you can trust me on this one, folks.**

You can *also* trust me when I tell ya that the new and drastically improved sound is more potent than a broken beer bottle heaved at your bobbing peroxide head. Purists may be peeved that a few songs get fiddled around with by fading up a few new multi-tracks in lieu of the older ones—most notably during the guitar passages on "Kill City"—but no matter how much you may have the original vinyl version burned into your brain, I guaranteed that your noggin will gladly accept these new values after only a few rotary motions. And while we're talking about the title track, it behooves me to point out that the handclaps now crack as crisply as a snappin' slave ship whip while the ragged backing vocals actually have a dissipated

Exile On Main St. edge to them. Oh, and did I forget to mention the barely audible part of the proceedings wherein an agitated Igg apes Williamson's unreasonably abrasive guitar fills with his own inimitable imitative vocal screech just before he begins the vocals? I thought not.

As for the rest of the album, from the sax-soaked *noir* ballad of inoperable obsession "Johanna" to the clued-up cautionary street-walkin' tale "Sell Your Love," *Kill City* remains an achingly *mature* work that eschews the brainy turn-of-phrase lyrics and brutal turn-of-stomach music of *Raw Power* in favor of a far more thoughtful and elegiac eleven step program of sanity survival.

And if things didn't quite work out exactly as planned, don't fault the two primary participants because they gave it their best shot while laboring under a stacked deck of circumstances that would've crushed lesser mortals like you and I into dust. That both James Williamson and Iggy Pop not only managed to subsequently survive, but successfully thrive, only proves that they *are* the greatest.

THE ALBUMS REVIEWED
THE WEIRDNESS

Reunions suck. School reunions. Work reunions. Drinkin' buddy reunions. Old girlfriend reunions. They're all just futile exercises in forlorn nostalgia about the so-called "good old days" when you were younger, faster, smarter, leaner, hungrier. And then one day, decades later, you meet up once again with your old cronies only to see them reflecting back the way you really are now: older, slower, stupider, fatter, lazier.

But when it comes to drastically diminished returns and disgustingly deflated expectations, the absolute worst—and unfortunately most prevalent—reunion of them all is the dreaded *rock band reunion* because there ain't nothing sadder than watching a buncha old geezers who used to be too cool for school now playing the fool. Soupy sez: Show me a disbanded band and I'll show you an ill-advised rock 'n' roll reunion, because there isn't a single legendary combo on the planet that hasn't at one time or another worshipped at the altar of avarice and cravenly cashed in to make one last fast back catalogue buck. Chisel their names on a cenotaph to cupidity because they're *all* crass casualties: Beatles, Who, Zeppelin, Pistols, Sabbath, Queen, Police, Genesis, Velvets, Dolls, Kiss, *ad museum piece nauseam*.

So when I heard that the original three Stooges were going to reunite and record their first new studio album in well-nigh forty years, I yawned and went back to sleep. Sure they managed to get a good head of steam going on their *Live In Detroit* reunion video, but if I had a bottom dollar for every band that can squirt on stage only to shoot blanks in the studio, I'd come back and buy this town and give it all, give it all to you.

An even more foreboding omen is that most of Iggy's post-Stooges solo albums after *The Idiot* and *Lust For Life* have been mediocre mail-in jobs which barely met the FDA's recommended daily minimum dose of rock 'n' roll. Iggy even admitted as much when he threw in the towel and conceded defeat on his very first solo album by bemoaning: "Well things have been tough without the Dum Dum Boys. I can't seem to speak the language."

But since you need more than two players to field a team, let's revise the above-noted starting lineup to also include *New Values, Party*, and *Soldier*. Even if you pencil in the antiseptic Pistolero metallo of *Instinct* as a designated hitter, that's still a pretty skimpy overall batting average for a professional who's been in the major leagues all his life. Because even the staunchest Igg adherent would be hard-pressed to call up farm team flops like *Blah Blah Blah* or *Brick By Brick*. Yet despite repeatedly benching himself while playing solo, Iggy always became Jimmy Hustle whenever he was a member of the Detroit Stooges. But the big question on every seasoned tout's mind was: Could Iggy come out of the dugout and do it again after being on the disabled list for so long?

The answer lies deep within this mesmerizing miasma which first envelops and then totally engulfs. If *The Stooges* is their pioneering prototypical punk rock album, *Funhouse* their idiot savant garde jazzbo album, and *Raw Power* their holocaustic laser-guided metal manifesto, then *The Weirdness* is the Asheton-Osterberg Overdrive's genetically customized hybrid of all three. One could even make a strong case for it being a punched up 'n' stripped down estranged distant cousin to *Kill City*, the missing link long player that Iggy recorded in 1975 with James Williamson and the Sales brothers.

This is the Motor City muscle machine that *American Caesar* should've been: a rumbling force to be reckoned with that'll smoke you every time, because under its hood lies a tightly coiled beast impatiently

waiting to be unleashed. *The Weirdness* represents a level of artistic and, yes, *literary* achievement the likes of which Iggy hasn't attained in decades. Listen carefully to the lyrics of "O Solo Mio" and you'll realize that this ain't no punch-drunk palooka talking: it's the learned words of a man who's been loitering with intent long enough to know what's what. More importantly, it's a bravura performance that's anchored by the solid workmanship of the Ashetons and Mike Watt on bass. Admirably eschewing any solos, they studiously hew the cobblestone path that Iggy walks barefoot on, his feet bleeding with each tortured step.

But just to prove that *The Weirdness* isn't all philosophical musings, here are a few random highlights from the rest of the album:

- Ron's corrosive trademark wah-wah which punctuates "You Can't Have Friends."

- Realizing that Iggy's "idea of fun" has the "killing" effect of *annoying* everyone.

- Iggy's uncanny spot-on impersonation of Jim Dandy Mangrum on "She Took My Money" which ends in a "1970" style soniclysm replete with repeated exhortations of "BLOW!" to veteran Stooges sax man Steve Mackay.

- The "Shake Appeal" handclaps which keep time on "Greedy Awful People" while Ron lets loose with a truly psychotic neural-fusing wah-wah solo.

- Iggy débuting an adenoidal paranoid voice we've never heard before on "Claustrophobia" when he literally wails: "Get out or I'll call the caw-hawps! I used to beat you a-huh-hup!"

- The ghost sax solo buried in the mix on "Trollin' " which barely bleeds through right after Iggy drawls: "Lookin' for . . . *somethin'* ."

- Iggy's riotous ad-libs during "I Wanna Be Your Man" which dissolve into a gnarled ruin of prototypical indecipherable Stoogespeak.

Ask any fight doctor and he'll tell you that rubber-legged pugs get K.O.'d all the time; that's why it takes a special breed of bruiser to get up off the canvas at the count of nine and then confidently beat down all comers until he's the last man standing.

This is the rock 'n' roll album you've been waiting over thirty-five years for, whether you know it or not. It isn't just another routine rock 'n' roll reunion record, it's what rock 'n' roll is *supposed* to be. It's about having *gumption*. And if you don't *like* it, then you haven't *listened* to it long enough. And if you *haven't* listened to it long enough, then you'll *never* understand why The Stooges are the last band standing and *still* the undisputed reigning heavyweight champions of rock 'n' roll.

Have *you* got the gumption?

THE ALBUMS REVIEWED
READY TO DIE

IGGY AND THE STOOGES   READY TO DIE

Now listen up and listen good, pilgrim. Just because I'm the sanctioned storyteller of these here Stooges doesn't mean that I'm on their payola payroll by a long shot, no suh! Which means, speaking of long shots, that I would have liked nothing better than to lift my leg on this album and let it blurt 'til it hurt.

But seein' as how I already left a load leaking down that limpoid new David Bowie disc, maybe it's just as well that I'm all spunked out because, strangely believe it, this new 40th Anniversary Edition *ain't all that bad* even if parts of it *do* give you a flaccid flashback, just like the album title itself does, in a "Feel Like I'm Fixin' To Die" way.

F'rinstance:

The striking Jimmie "Dyn-O-Mite" Walker front cover tribute pose that the singer strikes is an unabashed updated take on Todd Rundgren's advert for his seminal *Something/Anything?* album. You know, that'd be the one wherein Todd has a big wad of fused TNT in one hand and a lit match in the other while the caption dares the consumer to: Go ahead. Ignore me.

Then, when the singer pseudo snarls on "Gun" (which ain't the John Cale ditty): "If I had a fuckin' gun, I could shoot at everyone" it's an admirable alternate angle on Bill Wyman's 1974 neighborhood threat: "I'd like to get me a gun and scare the shit out of everyone."

Later, when the singer advises during the same song

that: "Money is a waste of time, 'course I made sure I got mine!" is it anywhere nearly as sagacious as when he used to squirt out such pearls of jizzdom as: "I'm healthy as a horse. Ah, but everything is spinnin' " or "I am your crazy driver. Honey, I'm sure to steer you wrong"? Perhaps not, but as any aging porn star will tell you: coming close is better than not coming at all—and there's more than enough spew stew left in them thar lizardo loins to thoroughly goo you through.

That's mainly because of the meat packers who provide the purée that propels this pud, namely: James Williamson on axe-o-rama, Steve Mackay on honky tonk saxophonics, Pedro Watt on basso profoundo, and the star of our show, the baddest criminal at large in the power house, the legendary Stooges co-founder, the truly irreplaceable Scott "Rock Action" Asheton, who's *still* skillfully slammin' the skins into submission like there's no tomorrow.

But there's always a yesterday, so don't you worry 'bout a thing if the beginning of "Job" reminds you of the beginning of "Loose" because that ain't no grand theft audio, that's nothing less than a heartfelt Jamesonian Institution tip of the skull to all the past blitzkrieg battle campaigns that Stoogestaffel Field Marshal Ron Asheton (ret.) led—and if you don't believe me that it's a crêpe-draped tribute of the highest new order, then all you have to do is just listen to how the aching ode "The Departed" ends and *see* if you don't end up shedding a tear or two.

However, lest you think that this dust up is little more than a summer rerun, I'm pleased as punch to report that things *really* heat up during the second half, starting with a title track that breaks new sonic soil with a radically different murky Stoneswagger that's never been heard on a Stoogeplatter before.

Then that's followed up with the pulchritudinous Russ Meyer top heavy tribute "DD's" which sounds as if it was recorded at Stax—if you catch my upper balcony drift. When the singer ain't too proud to beg that: "I'm on my knees for those double Ds," he's giving the Flat Chest Society a much-needed antidote to Rod Stewart's intolerant anti-implant anthem "Silicone Grown."

Look, I could continue waxing euphonic about how fantoonie this sonic sizzler is, but your time would be far better spent spinning it instead, if only so you can hear the singer rhyme "friendship" with "death trip" on the final track.

And they call *Dylan* a poet.

THE ALBUMS REVIEWED
IGGY'S GREATEST COMMERCIALS

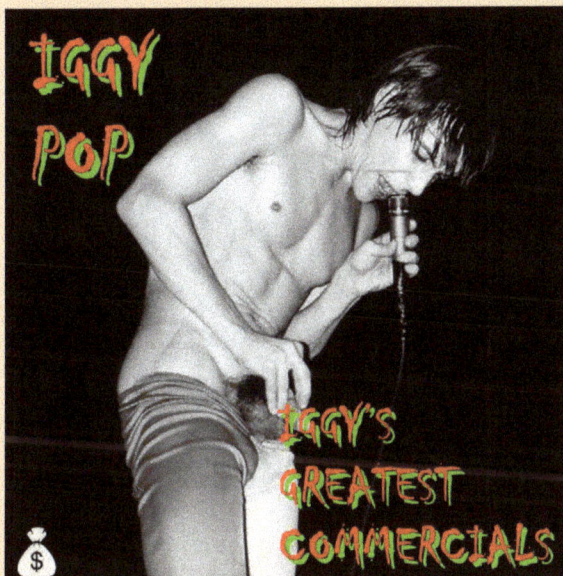

Ever since he signed with Gene $immons' record label, Iggy's career has been one long concrete kissing belly flop into the shallow end of the consumerism pool. So it comes as no surprise that this craven cash grab opens up with "Lust For Life Insurance!" and then spews out every other crass commercial from Iggy's sixty second song book, including ads for:

Raw Power Energy Drinks!
Shake Appeal Body Spray!
Penetration Condoms!
Death Trip Funeral Parlors!
I Wanna Eat Your Dog Food!
Cock In My Pocket Vibrators!
Skull Ring Tones!
Mexican Guy Immigration Lawyers!
I Need More Credit Loans!
Blah Blah Blah Phone Cards!
ATM Bank Machines!
Eggs On Plate Frozen Dinners!
Sell Your Love Escorts!
I Got A Right Legal Services!
Tight Pants Jeans!
Trollin' GPS Units!
Heavy Liquid Plumber!
Gimme Some Skin Moisturizer!
Head On Auto Repair!
I Need Somebody Matchmakers!
Wet My Bed Diapers!
She Took My Money Divorce Attorneys!
T.V. Eyeliner!
Your Pretty Face Is Going To Hell Beauty Salons!

Has the man *no* shame?

SHEPARD AND THE STOOGES

"You know who Shepard Fairey is, right?" It was more of a statement than a question when Robert said it during one of our weekly marathon two hour phone conversations in 2009.

"Sure," I immediately replied, confirming his assumption. "André The Giant Has A Posse. I'm a big fan of Shepard's work."

"That's good because he's a huge *Raw Power* fan and we've been working on a few things together. I'll send you one of them when we get off the chatterline."

Shortly thereafter, I received a file tagged "Stooges_dooji_Fairey-Matheu" that was the preliminary design for a new Stooges single, with the front cover being a skillful Skull-altering iteration of Robert's iconic Ford Auditorium photo, rendered in the classic Fairey style. Obviously that cravenly edited version of "Doojiman" was never officially released by Sony as originally planned, but the entire concept would later be lifted and admirably made

manifest with the song's full uncensored release as "hombre de negro" on *iguana de famosa banda - etiqueta negra de lugo*.

So when I found "Stooges_dooji_Fairey-Matheu" in my archive while assembling this book, I contacted Obey Giant for approval to publish it for the first time, accompanied by a 2010 essay that Shepard had written about The Stooges which was on his website.

And although I was granted authorization to use the artwork, I was denied permission to reprint the online essay because Shepard would prefer to write something new about *Raw Power* for the book as an Afterword and, oh, would I like to have high resolution scans of all his Stooges art as well?

So my sincere thanks go out to Vanthi Nguyen, Ajani Purnell, Angel Enciso, and Victoria Yarnish at Obey Giant for generously enabling all this to happen.

IGGY AND THE STOOGES
DOOJIMAN

82

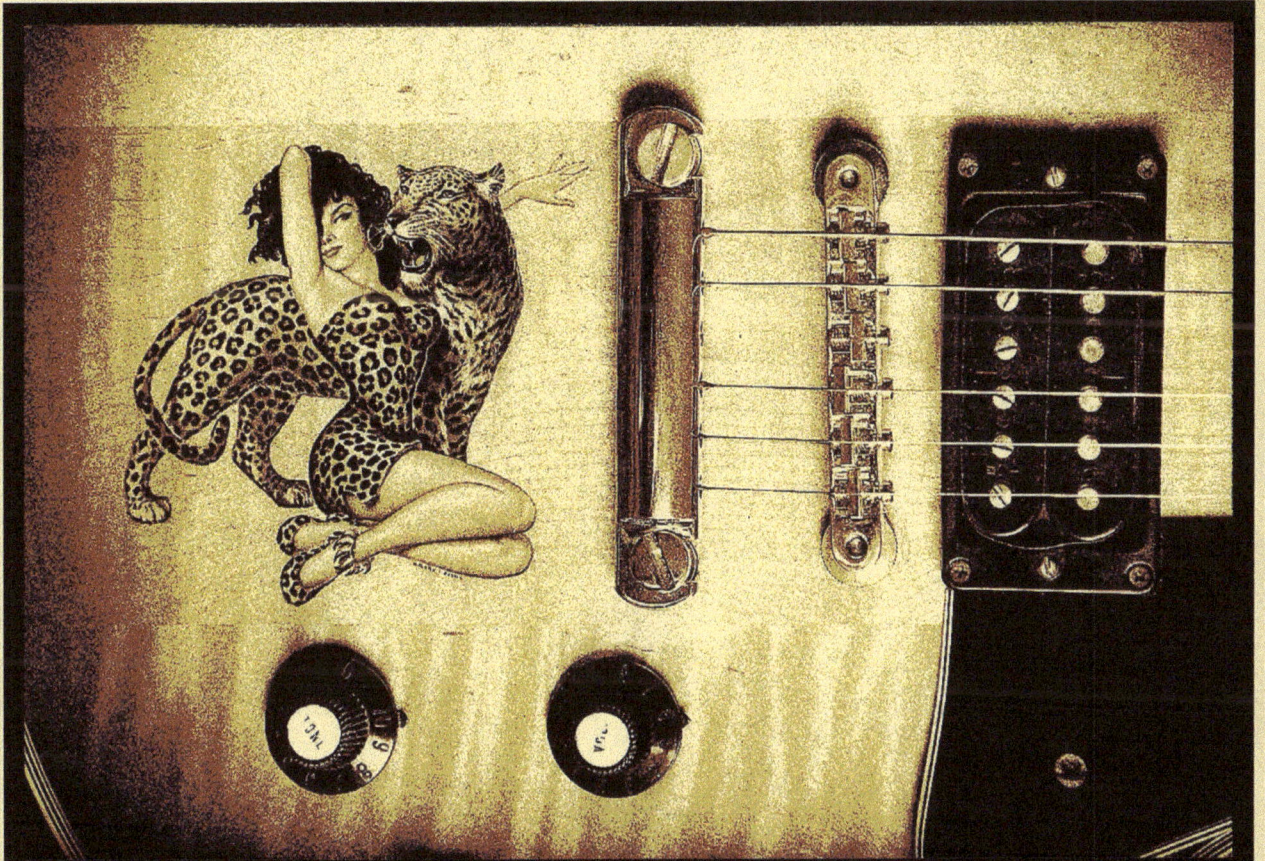

DOOJIMAN

SONY N SHIT

BLAH BLAH BLAH IPSUM E PLURIBUS UNUM SCHUNUM LEBERTY AND JUSTICE FOR A FEE   BLAH BLAH BLAH IPSUM E PLURIBUS UNUM SCHUNUM LEBERTY AND JUSTICE FOR A FEE
BLAH BLAH BLAH IPSUM E PLURIBUS UNUM SCHUNUM LEBERTY AND JUSTICE FOR A FEE   BLAH BLAH BLAH IPSUM E PLURIBUS UNUM SCHUNUM LEBERTY AND JUSTICE FOR A FEE

IGGY AND THE STOOGES

RAW POWER

SEARCH & DESTROY

JAMES WILLIAMSON   MISTER IGGY POP

C2SV FESTIVAL

SAN JOSE, CA
SEPTEMBER 28, 2013

JUST A COUPLE OF WELL- MANNERED BOYS

Iggy Pop and Robert Matheu Play it Safe

Two weeks after the Stooges book came out in October 2009, both Robert and Iggy appeared on New York public radio station WNYC to tell their side of the authorized and illustrated story. The following conversation appears courtesy of WNYC and was initially transcribed and edited for this new edition by myself using the original 2009 interview tape that Robert gave me a few days after it was recorded. This manual transcription was then cross-checked for further accuracy against the new official transcript that WNYC made for me in 2023.

My sincere thanks go to Lorraine Mattox, the Listener Services Director at New York Public Radio; and Andy Lanset, the Director of Archives at New York Public Radio for their assistance.

The reader will note how the entire conversation focuses around the book's creation and contents as if it were exclusively a photography book and not, as per the title, an illustrated biography. Indeed, not a single word is ever uttered about the writing contained within, leading one to conclude that the book hadn't been read by the host prior to its being discussed on the air.

Then again, I did write at the very beginning of the biography that: "Those of you who have heard this oft-told tale before are cordially invited to push pause and peruse the pretty pictures instead," so perhaps he took me at my word. Most people do.

JOHN SCHAEFER: This is *Soundcheck*, I'm John Schaefer. When the song "1969" hit the airwaves in the year 1969, the band that created it was widely dismissed as a bunch of under-talented weirdos. Well, 40 years later, "1969" is considered an American classic and the band, The Stooges, are hailed as pioneers of American Punk. In fact, they were just nominated to the Rock And Roll Hall Of Fame for the eighth time. Now, a new book of photography retraces the steps of the influential group. Entitled *The Stooges: The Authorized And Illustrated Story*, it documents the band from their formation in the late '60s to their 1975 breakup and then onward to their 2003 reunion. To talk about the book, I'm joined in the studio by Stooges frontman Iggy Pop and the book's main photographer, Robert Matheu. Iggy, welcome back.

IGGY POP: Hi, John, nice to be here.

JOHN: Bob, congratulations on the book—

ROBERT MATHEU: Thank you.

JOHN: —which has on this page, a revelation, a photograph of you, Iggy Pop, performing in a shirt. It has, in fact, happened and it has been captured on celluloid forever.

IGGY: It's happened more often than anyone suspects. I'm ready for the LA Philharmonic and when Dudamel wants me to come out to do some Stooges numbers there, I'm available.

JOHN: So the Philharmonic versions of Stooges songs, you're okay with. That's a Hollywood Bowl thing.

IGGY: As long as they sell, uh, my dog. [*laughter*]

JOHN: Now Bob, this is the first authorized book about The Stooges. Whose idea was this and why now?

ROBERT: I think it was a mutual idea. I think Iggy inspired me to do it. We were looking at old photographs. There was some old photographs that I discovered and passed them on to him and he hadn't seen them for a while. We were talking about this earlier and it just kind of grew out of . . . I knew there was a lot of photos that we hadn't seen that got shoveled, you know, underneath the carpet or pushed aside and it was just . . . I'd done a CREEM book previously about CREEM magazine and archived it. So during that process I started archiving and collecting more Stooges things and they were starting to turn up. And there was so many . . . After the first two albums, there was a lot of different incarnations of the bands with band members changing and coming and going and a lot of the photos started coming to me and pretty much telling me they needed a home, I suppose.

JOHN: So they're not all your photos, there's photos by Mick Rock and Leni Sinclair and lots of others. How did the editorial process between the two of you guys work?

ROBERT: He gave me free reign on it.

IGGY: Yeah, I had nothing . . . Neither I or the group have any business interest or editorial input into this book whatsoever.

JOHN: So you authorize it and then let him get about—

IGGY: I let him get the job done.

ROBERT: They'd answer questions if I came upon something I was unsure of and—

IGGY: You know what happened really was when the group re-emerged or exhumed ourselves . . . [*laughter*] As our heads emerged from our respective graves, as it were, the—

JOHN: I thought you were going to end that sentence with a very different noun. Thank you for that.

IGGY: No, no, no. I think all sorts of people started taking a second look at this group and our music started cropping and popping up in different places and Bob . . . Suddenly, I would guess, that suddenly Bob, who had been shooting Les Paul or the Red Hot Chili Peppers, found himself forty years later going to Stooges gigs again. And then, of course, you're gonna look through the old stuff, and I think that was probably how it started.

And somewhere along the line, he was hanging out with the rhythm section in my group, which is a good sign because they usually go for more of the glam, you know. And he was contributing photos to what we do now that were knowledgeable of the grit, the real deal. So I got used to that. We did a session with him or a couple of sessions in there and they went well. And then what really got me going was he gave me a couple of very old photos of us when we were all about twenty years old, eight I think. And I had—

JOHN: Had you ever seen them before?

IGGY: Not to my knowledge.

JOHN: Not to your knowledge.

ROBERT: This is as good an answer as I'll expect to get.

IGGY: And I got excited. And basically, as he . . . as it developed that he was gonna to do a book, then it developed that I was being . . . You know: "Would you authorize it? Would you be . . ." And I said: "Well, let me sign off on it."

JOHN: So what were those pictures that got you so excited?

IGGY: Well, they're the ones, the very early ones that . . . they're us in that . . . just in that old house, right at the beginning of the book when we're very close, right? When we're very very young.

JOHN: Early on in the book, there's—

IGGY: We were worth 125 bucks a night then. We were playing for free most weekends at the Unitarian Church, which you can see on the posters.

JOHN: Where is this? Is this back in Michigan—

IGGY: Ann Arbor. Ann Arbor, Michigan. And I just have a great affection for those photos and I just started to realize: "My God." It also, it . . . I noted that it also looked like any indie band in the sub-SoCal explosion; any indie band in the Seattle explosion; any indie band in the Sonic Youth, neo New York ex—

JOHN: Absolutely. And a lot of the bands at CBGB's in the mid-'70s.

IGGY: —plosion; all the Northampton, Mass. bands. And I thought: "Oh, my God, this really relates." And bing bang boom, there was a book.

ROBERT: And so much of that had been celebrated before, but The Stooges had never been celebrated or presented in that fashion.

JOHN: Let me read you guys a comment that comes from Peter in Sunset Park. Sort of going, Iggy, to what you were just saying. There are so many American bands, Australian bands, bands around the world that treat Iggy And The Stooges as their template for music. He goes on to mention Mudhoney, The Fluids, dozens of Australian punk bands. What does Iggy Pop think of this level of worship? Is it flattering to have hundreds of bands cover and rip off "T.V. Eye" or does it get annoying?

IGGY: Ha ha ha ha. Well, gee, that's about a 50/50. It's a sandwich. [*laughter*] It's a sandwich, dude.

JOHN: Bob, Iggy must be a photographer's dream.

ROBERT: Yeah, indeed, and he was—

JOHN: The wild antics on stage.

ROBERT: He had mentioned about when they came back in 2003 and playing again. I was excited, obviously, to have them back out there because still, to this day—and I shot a performance in Toronto last summer—I still never know what to expect and I'm still capturing different moments and different elements. Plus, since I have so much of a history with them already and have a few classic images of them, I'm always looking for something different than that; try to get something that I haven't captured before. He still delivers, still delivering.

JOHN: There's a couple of striking photos of the current incarnation of Iggy and The Stooges where, like, every vein on Iggy's chest . . .

ROBERT: Oh, yeah, the Reading Festival in 2005.

JOHN: Is that where that was?

ROBERT: Yes.

JOHN: Really striking stuff. And part of the work that you've done with Iggy and the revised, the reunited band, is the cover art for *The Weirdness* which was the most recent album. Iggy, there's a foreword by Alice Cooper in the book where he ends by sort of bemoaning the fact that people never got the humor in his music or in your music. I mean, when you look back at some of those old songs, do you understand how people might have missed, whatever, you know, the wit, the undercurrent of subversive humor that there was there?

IGGY: We were threatening to certain people's jobs, frankly. There was a, or they thought, there was a new—

JOHN: Who were those people?

IGGY: The Woodstock elite was coming in and there was going to be a certain . . . there was going to be a new industry formed with the glow of a . . . bathed in the glow of LSD and paid for by the youth consumer, who was going to be led in a certain way. And then, all of a sudden, you had biker gangs, runaways in Haight-Ashbury—and people like The Stooges saying: "Okay, we're here, we're ready to love!" and then lookin' around and saying: "Hey, this isn't what you told me. This isn't for real." But there was, there was a lot of humor in what we were doing and some people, people who were relaxed with the group, were able to

get it and particularly ninth, tenth, eleveth-grade kids got it right away with no problem.

JOHN: Even if they didn't understand as a nine, ten, or I don't remember which of those grades I was in at the time but, you know, the whole idea, you know, the nuclear bomb and the napalm and all the, you know, the violent imagery and some of the songs were just so over the top that, you know, you wondered how anybody took this seriously.

IGGY: It was over the top within the context of formal poetry, but it was nothing but absolutely the normal every day reality that the world was livin' at the time. I got those lyrics out of a *Time* magazine piece on the . . . A very real war was going on and killin' a bunch of people but, you know, when I say there's humor in the group, I mean that we're one of the few groups who would let humor happen when it confronted us. There's nothing more pompous in the world today than rock. You know, go listen to Mahler. [*laughter*]

JOHN: To get away from the pomposity, you want to go to Mahler.

IGGY: Well, no, this is what I'm saying is, I know Mahler, right? So I'm saying, you know, you're actually better off, you know. So yeah, at least there's a melody; counterpoint, you know.

JOHN: How's that happened to rock? How's it gotten to that?

IGGY: Well, first of all, the role was removed.

JOHN: The role . . .

IGGY: The role was removed. So first you had rock and roll and you had rock and then . . . you really did, right? There was a period in the '80s where things were still rocking and I thought . . . And then it was: "Tonight, you and eighty-five thousand other wage slaves will bow your heads, become neo-vegetarians and rock your way into a stadium near you, to pay what you're told, to listen to what you've already heard too many times on every possible inlet and outlet." You know, and . . . Yecch.

JOHN: Speaking of having heard things too many times, there's a great picture on the back, Bob, of your book. Is this one, this must be one of yours 'cause it's a recent, relatively recent . . . The back cover of the book is just a piece of paper taped to the floor of the stage and there's a foot on a guitar pedal.

IGGY: That's Ron's foot.

JOHN: That's . . . the late Ron Asheton . . .

IGGY: The late Ron, the late great Ron.

ROBERT: Yeah, the wah-wah pedal.

DOG
TV EYE
1970
FUNHOUSE/LA
SKULL RING
TROLLIN'
MY IDEA of FUN
SHE TOOK MY $
IM FRIED
ATM
NO FUN

JOHN: The piece of paper is the set list for that night's concert. Some of the old songs, "T.V. Eye" . . . "Dog" presumably is "I Wanna Be Your Dog" . . .

IGGY: Yes.

JOHN: No "Lust For Life." Now, is that going back, Iggy, to what you were just saying, that, you know, I don't want to play a song that you've heard on a gazillion commercials, or do you see—

IGGY: No, it just wasn't appropriate for that group. That's all. It just wasn't the right song for that.

JOHN: Because it wasn't a Stooges song.

IGGY: It wasn't . . . It . . For the . . . For the core . . . For that particular group, uh, it wasn't, it wasn't right.

JOHN: Okay. The book is called *The Stooges: The Authorized And Illustrated Story*. Bob, a lot of . . . some of your pictures, a lot of the oldest pictures from the other photographers that you've sort of edited into this, you're going back over 30, almost . . . you are going back forty years. Has the state of rock photography, rock and roll photography changed?

ROBERT: Oh, yes, yes. Yeah, considerably.

JOHN: How?

ROBERT: Well, there's boundaries and there's politi— There's not as much freedom to it of going to the event and having that freedom to move around or do this and that. You know, we got security guards there all the time to protect the group from the audience or whatever. The Stooges, on the other hand, they invite the audience up on stage.

JOHN: I was just going to say, The Stooges, back in the day, you'd have to have those guys protecting the audience from the band.

ROBERT: The picture on the back cover of Ronnie's foot, and the setlist, as you said, was during the stage invasion and during "No Fun" and the whole audience gets up and participates, and Ron would usually take his pedals and retreat behind the amps for safety.

IGGY: Yes.

ROBERT: And I wanted to kinda capture . . . Well, there's pictures in the book like that, too. You could see the saxophone player running double duty, he's holding the amps up, you know, like Ron's soloing, so . . .

JOHN: How did you originally gain acc— I mean, how did you guys first meet?

ROBERT: Uh, probably as his solo career started up, I was starting to turn professional and I was still in Detroit, working in Detroit, and I would do this. He'd go to radio stations to do interviews, and I'd . . . The

record company hired me to tag along and, you know, back then I would just, like, blend it into the woodwork. I was the fly on the wall, not to be intrusive. I just kept going to his solo shows over the years and stayed in touch, as he said, with the drummer and stay in touch with the band.

IGGY: That's very wise.

JOHN: Staying in touch with the drummer.

IGGY: Very wise. There's underrated . . . People don't get it when it comes to music and it's all about the drummer. Always is.

JOHN: Spoken like an ex-drummer.

IGGY: Well, there you go. [*laughter*]

JOHN: Although that was pretty far back in your—

IGGY: All right.

JOHN: In fact, the first picture inside the book, Bob, is not of Iggy, but of Ron, the late Ron Asheton. It's this really funny picture of him with his sunglasses up on his forehead, and he's got the beer and the cigarette in the holder, and he's kinda like . . . you know, glaring down at the camera with a, sort of, bemused look on his face. Um, he died in January.

ROBERT: Right.

JOHN: Obviously, during the period when this book would've been coming together.

ROBERT: We had put the book in the works a year ago, August. Everyone was, you know, cognizant of . . that we were going to do this. And actually, the day that I found out that Ronnie had passed away, I'd just gotten my final contract from the book publisher. I was signing it that day, and I was also supposed to be leaving that night to go to Ann Arbor to sit down with Ronnie and start going over some stories and look at photos and all that. So he'd contributed quite a bit to me to what the vision should be beforehand. And Iggy called me at one point in January when I was gettin' the first layouts done and I told him, I said: "Ron has a very big presence in this book just by his mere absence right now," and because the way the layout just came, it just punctuated it throughout.

JOHN: So it's . . . But . . . There he is. Pride of place—

ROBERT: Yeah, it was a very good thing.

JOHN: —ment inside the book. Iggy, just to get away from the book for a moment, I mentioned in the beginning of the segment that you guys, you and The Stooges, have been nominated, for the eighth time, to the Rock And Roll Hall Of Fame. Are you sick of the

suspense at this point?

IGGY: No. I don't have a . . . sick isn't the word. There's no . . . neither sickness nor suspense are present.

JOHN: Do you . . . does it matter to you, uh— You know, if elected, would you serve? Would you show up?

IGGY: Oh, well, of course, it's . . . it's always, uh, it's . . . it's always nice at this stage of the game to be invited to the party but, uh, if . . . if not, I understand that we'll set some sort of a record, apparently. Apparently we'll be the most rejected . . . [*laughs*]

JOHN: Which somehow seems appropriate for Iggy And The Stooges.

IGGY: Yeah, right, so . . . you know.

JOHN: The book is called *The Stooges: The Authorized And Illustrated Story*. And the book's main photographer, Bob Matheu, will be doing a sign— Will you both be at the signing tonight?

IGGY: Yes.

JOHN: Both Iggy Pop and—

IGGY: Uh, yeah, we're going to be in . . . Where are we?

JOHN: You're at Barnes & Noble in Tribeca—

IGGY: Yes, yes we are.

JOHN: —at seven o'clock.

IGGY: Thank you.

JOHN: That'll do it for today's show.

BOY IN OHIO

On January 18th 1974, armed with a Kodak Instamatic camera, Jeff Magnum photographed The Stooges playing "Search And Destroy" from a fourth row seat at the Allen Theatre in Cleveland.

Three years later in 1977, armed with a Guild Jet Star II bass, he was playing "Search And Destroy" with the Dead Boys in front of packed crowds at CBGB's in New York and all across North America and the United Kingdom on their *Young Loud And Snotty* tour.

"The Stooges opened for Slade, and they only played half an hour," Jeff remembers four decades later. "There were rumors flying around that night that Iggy did something like fourteen Tuinals and was all fucked up. But then they came on and totally kicked ass!"

Of course they did.
Was there any other choice?

IGGY POP FAN CLUB

MEMBERSHIP

Name Jeff Magnum

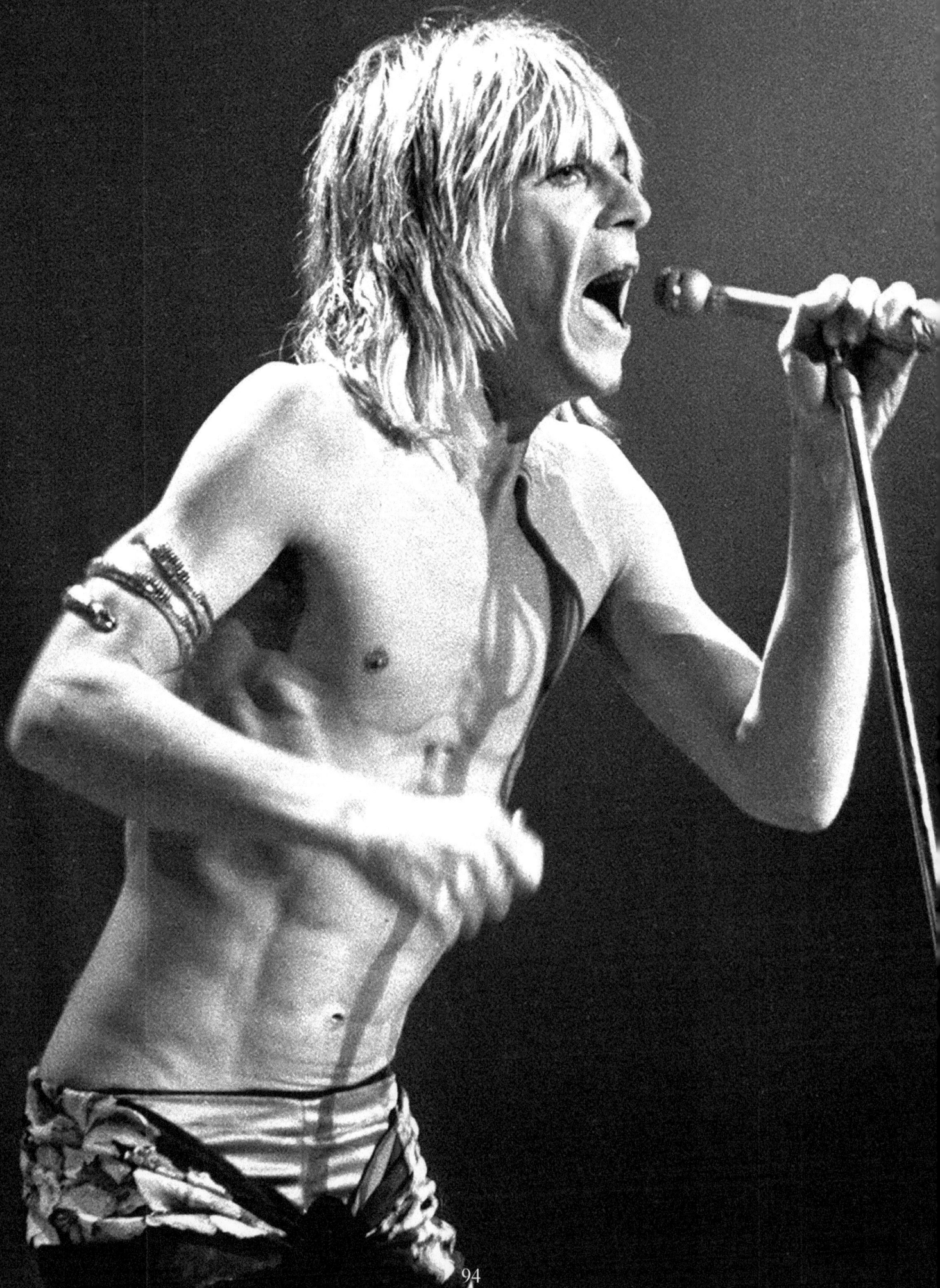

WARNING! CHOKING HAZARD

by **Robert Matheu**

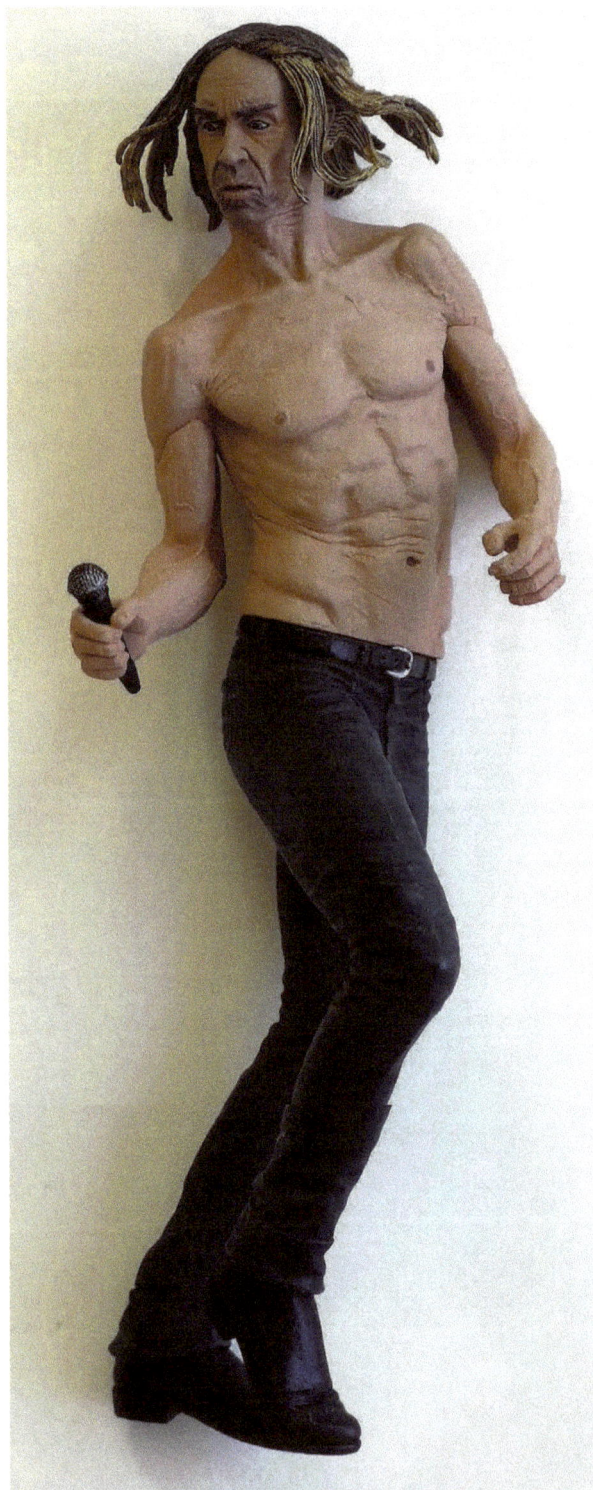

Just when you thought that *nothing* could possibly top the recent *Raw Power* projects, along comes this equally *über* Iggy Pop NECA action figure.

The iconic pose is based on this color photograph (opposite page) that I took of Iggy during the opening night of the band's London Hammersmith shows in 2010.

The meticulous fine detailing was then achieved by analyzing over one hundred *additional* photos of the UK shows to ensure authentic rock action exactitude from the pout of the snout all the way down to the inseams of the jeans.

Due to this abnormally high degree of anatomical accuracy, admittance is restricted to ages 14 and up.

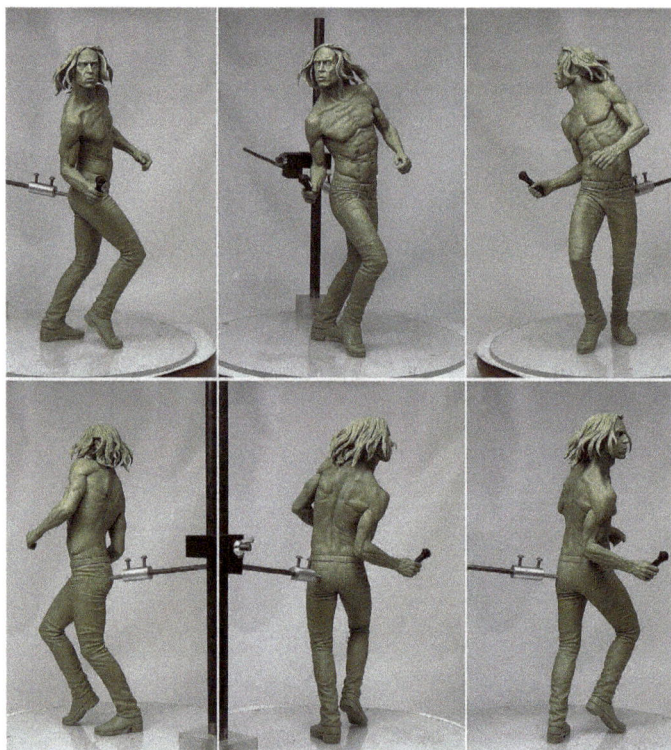

THIS IS ALICE SPEAKING

JEFFREY MORGAN: Hello.

ALICE COOPER: Hi Jeffrey, this is Alice.

JEFFREY MORGAN: Thank you for calling so we can talk about The Stooges.

ALICE: Oh, yeah, no problem at all. I mean, you know, it's the kinda thing where I kinda came up at the same time as Iggy and so, you know, I was watching this guy. When you're from L.A. or Phoenix and you go to Detroit and you're playing a big pop festival for the first time . . . I'd never heard of the MC5 before. I had never heard of Iggy And The Stooges and so those were the bands that were on this festival. And I'm watching the MC5 and I said: "Oh, these guys do a *show. This is great!*" I was so unused to seeing bands do shows. Y'know, Detroit bands did *shows*. And then I saw Iggy and I thought: "*What the hell?*"

JEFFREY: Well, that's what I was gonna ask because 2009 marks the fortieth anniversary of Alice Cooper.

ALICE: Right.

JEFFREY: And it also marks the fortieth anniversary of The Stooges. In 1969, anyone who saw the Alice Cooper Group knew that they were seeing something that they'd literally never seen before.

ALICE: Right. And that's the kind of thing that *this* was. *I* was even surprised!

JEFFREY: So that's your first memory of seeing The Stooges.

ALICE: Yeah, I saw them and I went . . . *Immediately*, you know, my competition gene rose up in me and I went: "*Oh*, here's an entity to be *dealt* with." Because, you know, *this* guy is . . . This, you know, very few . . . You know, I'd look at other bands and I'd go: "Okay, lead singer, so what, so what, so what, so what." Y'know, 'cause I was pretty used to getting the audience *totally shocked* by what *we* were doing and, you know, nobody had ever seen anything like *me* before. And then I saw somebody that *I* had never seen anything like before.

JEFFREY: So you knew, finally, what it was like for people to see *your* act.

ALICE: Yeah, and the best compliment I think I ever gave anybody was: Iggy's one of the only guys I wouldn't want to go on *after*.

JEFFREY: Well, that's what you always say. When you wrote the liner notes to the reissue of the first Stooges album, you wrote that they made a

permanent impression on you, but in what *way* did they make a permanent—

ALICE: I had never seen anybody . . . You know, first of all, there was no punk—or at least it wasn't *called* punk. I'd seen bands that were kind of raw bands before, that were kind of, you know, just *down*, and I'd just kinda look at them and go: "Ah, they're not very good." 'Cause I'm always looking for how good the guitar player is, and how good the songs are, and I could always just write them off as being crummy garage bands.

But then I heard this band that was *so basic* . . . and *knew it* to the point where they used it as a theatrical piece. The fact that they just stood there and just played those chords, those three chords . . . *with an attitude*. And then this guy, this lead singer, who was sort of like Mick Jagger's illegitimate love child, you know, was up there and he was *a total show* unto himself. So I said: "It *looks* like an accident . . . but I know it's *not* an accident." These guys had really created something that is *really* unique to anything that I had ever seen before.

JEFFREY: Well, like you were saying, you saw a lot of bands perform when you were just starting out.

ALICE: Yeah!

JEFFREY: Now how long did it take for you, and at what point, did you realize that The Stooges just weren't just another faceless band, but musicians who were operating *on the same level* as The Alice Cooper Group?

ALICE: It was . . . it was *totally different*. It was sorta like . . . To get the audience back after Iggy got on . . . This was back when he'd go in the audience, get in a fight with a Marine, get knocked out, they'd carry him back up on stage *bleeding*, he'd finish the song, he'd put peanut butter on himself—and still . . . no props! *He was the prop!* He was the theatrical prop of the band.

JEFFREY: So you knew *immediately* that—

ALICE: This guy was *really good* at what he did, and I just wondered if *he* knew how good he was. You know, *he* was not a magnificent singer and the *songs* were not magnificent songs, but they were *perfect* for that band. And I just got to the point where . . . I mean, I got addicted to "Loose" and "T.V. Eye" and "I Wanna Be Your Dog" to the point where—we did so many shows with them—that they were one of the only bands where I would say: "Hey, listen, we're going to see these dudes. I wanna see a couple of these songs." Generally I would just go: "Hey, I'm gonna stay in my dressing room and, you know, get ready for the show" 'cause I just didn't care. [laughs] But with The Stooges, I wanted to actually see the show!

JEFFREY: Because you never knew what might happen!

ALICE: Yeah, I was . . . Well, we worked with The Doors before and The Doors were like that, too. Y'know, The Doors had a thing for a while where you went there 'cause you didn't know what Jim was gonna do. You didn't know if Jim was gonna fall off the stage, you didn't know if he was gonna take twenty-five minutes to start the song. And honestly, most bands back then were a pretty much formulated thing. So when something came along new like that, you really wanted to see it. So working with The Doors was different, but working with The Stooges was entirely different.

JEFFREY: What are your thoughts on the fact that you and Iggy both knew and were influenced by Jim Morrison, and the different directions that you both took from that?

ALICE: Yeah, I think that . . . I mean, when I first saw

Morrison . . . The first time I heard him, I went: "This guy's an opera singer." You know . . . [singing] "When the mu-sic's o-vah . . ." I'm going: "What kind of voice is that?" I'm used to Mick Jagger. And then when I saw The Doors, I started listening to them and then, all of a sudden, this guy was not just the lead singer, he was, like . . . [pauses] He was like a poet. He was sort of, like a . . . He was almost like a Victorian poet. But he was this guy that was just . . . He was James Dean . . . He was all these guys rolled up into one. And totally unpredictable. There was nothing where you . . . You really couldn't put a moniker on the guy. He didn't do anything like anybody else.

The rest of the band, Robbie and the rest of the guys, were just great musicians and great players but they were smart enough, when it came to the show, to get out of the way of Jim. Let Jim be the show. Well, that's the same thing with Iggy. Get out of the way, let Iggy do the show.

JEFFREY: And basically, to me, it seems that you took the cerebral aspects of The Doors' performance and Morrison's psyche, and Iggy took the physical part.

ALICE: I think so, too. I see it as . . . That's exactly it. Iggy was always much more sexual than Alice Cooper when it came to, just, raw sex and down and dirty . . . Almost sort of like the ultimate hippie. You know: barefoot, torn up Levis, and no shirt—and has no problem with taking his pants off. Whereas Alice was sort of this elegant vampire. I wanted Alice to be the thing that was indescribable. Alice was sort of a surrealistic . . . He was a lead singer, but he was totally surrealistic. And again, I didn't want you to be able to compare me with anybody 'cause really, at that time, there really wasn't anybody to compare me with.

So when I saw a kindred spirit in Iggy, I just kind of smiled and went: "Okay, this is gonna be fun," because . . . It was a challenge! And everybody always wanted there to be a feud. Everybody always wanted there to be: Who's crazier? Alice or Iggy? Who did this and who did that? And then they started combining 'em, okay. Alice took a crap on stage and Iggy ate it. Or Iggy took a crap on stage and Alice ate it. Then they started combining the urban legends. [laughs]

JEFFREY: Didn't you and Iggy once go to Brian Wilson's house?

ALICE: Yeah!

JEFFREY: Iggy says he has no recollection of this. What do you remember of it?

ALICE: That was after the Grammy awards, and not only . . . I remember this so specifically because we were sitting there and he says: "I want you guys to come over." And it was me and Iggy and, I think, one of the guys from Three Dog Night, Danny Hutton. I think he was there, and somebody else. And we went

there—it might have been Bernie Taupin, I'm not sure—but we went there and we kept looking at each other going: "Right, now we're at Brian Wilson's house, this is amazing!"

And . . . he couldn't get the door open and he said: "Be very quiet, my kids are all asleep." And he couldn't get his key out, so he *broke* the window with a big rock. Then, of course, he went in and he brought his kid out, he was holding his [*laughs*] the baby by one leg, saying: "Look, this is my baby." It was *totally* crazy. And then he went down in the basement and he sits down at the piano and he says: "I'm gonna play you guys the greatest song ever written." And we sat there thinking: Well, that'll be good if Brian Wilson says . . . And then he starts playin' "Mammy's Little Baby Loves Short'nin' Bread." And he says: "I'm serious. This is technically the greatest song ever written." And you know, we sat there and went: "Okay."

And the cool thing was, he had in his basement a seventy-two track studio and he kept the master tapes of *Pet Sounds* on the board so you could *mix* it anyway you wanted to mix it.

JEFFREY: Just like they do now on the Internet.

ALICE: Yeah! So Iggy was on one . . . I had five or six faders down on one set, I had another one down here. Danny Hutton had a few down here. And we were mixing it the way *we* wanted to hear it. I pushed my fader up and all of a sudden you heard *dogs* barking and I said: "Where did *that* come from?" But that was

the toy. Everybody who came up there could mix *Pet Sounds*.

JEFFREY: I once asked Ted Nugent if he thought that his music would have been different in some way if he'd grown up in Chicago or New York as opposed to Detroit and he said he didn't think it would've mattered. He said that no matter where he'd grown up, what you saw now was probably what you would've got. Do *you* think The Stooges would've been the same had they been from another state other than Michigan?

ALICE: I honestly *don't* think so, unless . . . I think if it was from a Midwest state like Cincinnati, St. Louis, Chicago, Detroit, yeah. *But* . . . Detroit had that added sense of *danger* to it. Detroit had that, you know . . . We were all Detroit kids, we all grew up in Detroit. I mean, *I* grew up and it was always a very *dangerous* town. But it was also . . . The one thing about Detroit that was *very* unusual was that, *even now*, if you were from Detroit, you were *fraternity*. In other words, I can walk into a house full of rappers, who were the most dangerous guys in the world, and they'd look at me and I'd go: "Detroit" and they'd go: "Oh, okay." And it *was* okay. In fact, they'd probably *protect* you. Because you're a Detroit guy. There was always this fraternity of: *If you're from Detroit, you're okay*. You could walk into . . . My guys in my band, with hair down to their waist, could walk into the . . . probably the most dangerous bar in Detroit, where there's nothing but black guys that kill people for a living, and we would be fine. Because we're musicians and we're from Detroit. So you're okay.

JEFFREY: How do you feel about The Stooges now receiving the overwhelming recognition that they now enjoy, given the ups and downs that both you and Iggy have suffered through over the past four decades?

ALICE: I think the one thing that stayed consistent is that *we* stayed consistent. We might have gone through a lot with what happened in our lives, but I go see Iggy now and I think of what Alice does now, and it's *not that much different* from what we did in the beginning. I always stayed true to my theatrics and I always stayed true to the fact that I was in a hard rock band: two guitars, bass, drums.

The first thing that we would do, ninety percent of our show, was we would rehearse the music. Ninety percent. The other ten percent was the show. To me, you've got to be a *killer* rock band before you're a theatrical band. And I think The Stooges were the same kind of thing. They believed in that kind of music *so much*, that that's what they did. And if they ever started doing things other than what they do, I would be disappointed. I say the same thing about AC/DC. If they ever learn, like, three or four more chords, they wouldn't be AC/DC. [*laughs*]

JEFFREY: You spoke earlier about always looking for

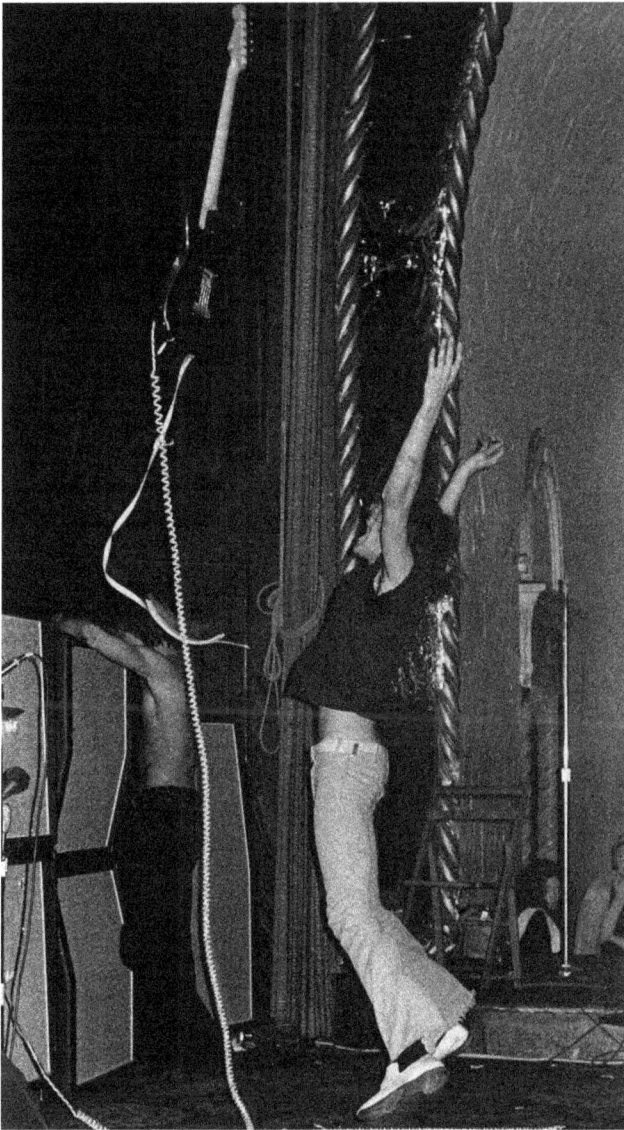

like a Steve Vai or a Jeff Beck, he really wouldn't have fitted in that band. I think he needed to be a *real punk* "I just like to play this kind of music" guitar player. He might . . . On his own, he might've been really, really good. I never heard him really just let out and play. But he never let me down, he never disappointed me when I saw him on stage.

JEFFREY: When I spoke with Lou Reed and Ron Mael back in the '70s, both of them bemoaned the fact that their audiences often didn't see the humor in what they were doing. Do you feel the same way?

ALICE: Yeah. I think a lot of people at that time missed the sense of humor in Alice Cooper and missed the sense of humor in Iggy. I think there definitely was a sense of humor to both bands that a lot of people missed. They saw us as being something that their *parents* hated and they saw us as being something they would like to *be* like . . . We were almost like characters that really didn't *belong* in this world. It was one of those things where . . . It was sort of like you were witnessing a couple of *monsters*, really. Iggy was unreal, I was unreal—and even *Ted Nugent* was unreal. When Ted would get on stage he was this unreal kind of *thing* up there. [*laughs*] And I think that was the thing about us that was great: the fact that we didn't *relate* to a lot of people.

JEFFREY: And a lot of people *still* can't relate to the three of you.

ALICE: Yeah, I *love* that!

how good the guitar player is. How does Ron Asheton fit into that line of thought?

ALICE: Ron Asheton was not easy to know. Ron Asheton was sorta like Glen Buxton. He was very similar to Glen Buxton, in the fact that he *wasn't* the life of the party. He was the guy that stood in the corner with his drink with his sunglasses on and his white boots, whatever he was wearing. He had a look that was very, very cool and he didn't say a lot and when he played, he played *within himself*, is what I like to say. He never tried to play something that he couldn't play. So he played totally within himself and he was *very satisfied* with what he played. I don't think we ever heard how *good* Ronnie could be, because the music didn't really go to that, it never really asked for him to be a great guitar player. I mean, as far as a lead player.

But, when you talk about keeping that thing . . . keeping that music down right to point . . . right to the *guts* of it, *that's* what he did. I just don't think that he was in the type of band where . . . If he was a *great* guitar player, probably . . . I mean, I'm talking about

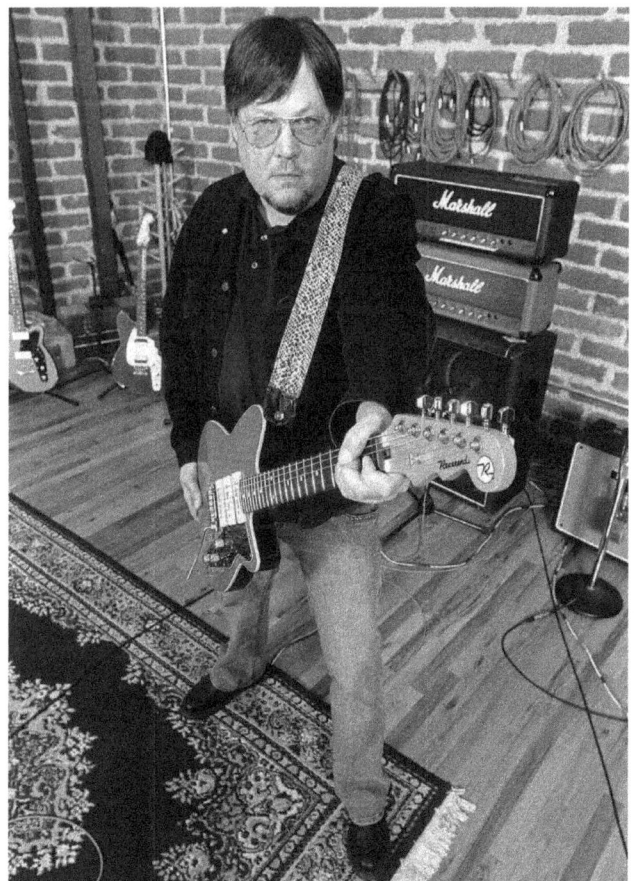

STOOGE WATCH

by **Brian J. Bowe**

Stooge Watch No. 1

::

December 2001

Yes, it's fantastic to hear that Iggy Pop has asked Ron and Scott Asheton to head into the studio for some good old-fashioned rock action. But let's not get our hopes up too high.

"It's pretty simple and straightforward," said Iggy's manager Art Collins. "Iggy's still signed with Virgin Records records and he's working on a new album. He called Ron and Scott and said: 'Hey, maybe you guys want to play on a couple tracks and see what comes out of it.' "

Iggy and the Ashetons have always remained friends, Collins said, and the brothers agreed to the sessions. But currently there's not even studio time booked. So it's a little early to ask if Ron can still fit into his old clothes.

Sure, we all want to see a Stooges reunion complete with tour. Especially now that these fellows are less apt to pass out on the bathroom floor with a spike in their veins before the show, or roll around in glass and bloody themselves, or throw peanut butter on the audience, or pull down their pants. But these things have a rhythm of their own, and we need to let them progress at their own pace.

"Towards the end of January we'll know more," Collins said. He cautioned fans against reading too much into the studio work. "It's not going to be some grand reunion. Or who knows, maybe it could be. But it's not the intent. It's just for them to get together and do a couple of tracks," he said. Maybe those rumblings are inspiring the ex-Stooges to mount up and ride again.

Stooge Watch No. 2
::
January 2003

Well, if it's not 1969, at least we know it's another year for me and you. The difference is this time, there's plenty to do.

The brothers Asheton are due to arrive in Miami the week of January 13th to record two tracks for Igg's new album, according to sources at Osterberg HQ. Reunion concerts have not been discussed yet and sources continue to insist that the studio work is the sole focus of the project. The record is set to be handed into Virgin Records March 31st for release later this year.

The only other surviving Stooge, James Williamson, is not participating in the project, management said. However, late bassist Dave Alexander is said to be watching over the sessions from whatever strange plane he inhabits these days.

It hasn't been revealed who is handling the bass chores. Stooge Watch recommends Mike Watt, who has been making a great study of The Stooges' *oeuvre* in recent years.

Stooge Watch No. 3

::

February 2003

Yes, their music may be raw, ferocious stuff. But never let it be said that The Stooges aren't gentlemen of honor, willing to come to the rescue of vulnerable creatures.

"I have a little power, and for something good, I'll use it," said Stooges guitarist Ron Asheton. And recently, he had to use that power to come to the aid of a stray cat that was being abused at the hands of some knife-wielding, feline-hating kitchen help in Miami Beach, Florida.

Ron and his brother Scott were in the Sunshine State to record some new tracks for Iggy Pop's upcoming Virgin release. And while the Stooge Watch desk has been breathlessly awaiting the results of those sessions, we were interested to hear more about this tale of heroism.

The scene was a place called the 11th Street Diner, near the Ashetons' hotel in Miami Beach. "Iggy took us there the first night," Ron said. "I was going there for my pre-studio food, and when we were done I'd go back. I was spending about $100 a day there. I loved the diner, and I was stuck on it."

Part of the diner's attraction was the food, part of the attraction was sitting on the patio, Ron said. But a big attraction was a stray orange-and-white cat with a crooked smile. "For me, that cat was part of making me go to the diner every night," Ron said.

The cat was shy and bore the telltale signs of the rough life of a street-walkin' cheetah. "Somebody had already kicked his head in once, so his face was kind of smashed," Ron said. "He's got a funny little smile."

But with patience and table scraps, the brothers were able to gain its trust. "My brother would finally get him to take a piece of ham out of his hand. I finally got to pet him, and people were saying 'Not many people get to pet him,' " Ron said.

So while he was in town, Ron took care of the stray, which he described as a "mascot" for the diner. "I'd bring him cat food and put it in his favorite spot," he said.

The night before Ron was coming back to Michigan, he found himself again dining with his brother. "All of a sudden, I hear scuffling and stuff, and I hear my brother saying 'Hey! Hey, don't do that,'" Ron said. The cat had gotten into the kitchen, and a couple of workers were chasing it. One picked up a knife, the other picked up a table, and both were threatening to kill the cat. Apparently, these guys were fucking with the wrong cat. They hadn't reckoned with Stooge Power.

"It was weird. I had to stop it," Ron said, saying that he and Scott jumped to action and let the would-be cat killers know they meant business. "Just my yelling, they just kind of slunked back into the diner."

Even though it was late at night, Asheton was so furious he had to call a good friend back home. "I was so angry that I called Dara. I was just raving, ranting about it, and she spread the word," Ron said, noting that Mike Watt and Thurston Moore were among those who were alerted and who spread the word.

Ron stressed that his beef is with the cat-abusing help, not the diner itself, which he still maintains is a cool place.

That experience was the only blotch on a great time, Ron said, noting that the sessions at the Hit Factory studio went well. The brothers wrote and recorded four new songs with Igg in less than ten days. "It turned out well. I'm happy with it," he said. "It's fun. Amazingly, all the basic tracks were, like, one take. It wasn't necessarily going to be that way, but that's how it turned out."

With all that history between them, Ron confessed that the initial rendezvous with Mr. Osterberg was a bit uncomfortable. "The first meeting was a little awkward," Ron said. "We were at the hotel and he came to meet us and it was a little strange. I felt a little nervous because I hadn't really seen him for twenty years. My brother had seen him, but I hadn't."

"I knew it was a little awkward for Iggy, too. But it melted away very quickly," Ron added. "And everyone relaxed. It was like old times. Iggy opened up and laughed a little more. At first he was all business. By the time we left the first trip, it was going fine." The band's fans won't be disappointed with the new songs, which have Ron playing guitar and bass on them.

"It's good and *Stooge*, so it's true to form. It's that nice raw sort of Stooges rock and roll," he said.

Stooge Watch No. 4
::
April 2003

The Stooges are returning to the stage on April 27th at the Coachella festival in the California desert. Not only that, they've selected the Stooge Watch's preferred bass player, Mike Watt.

Stooge Watch No. 5

::

May 2003

In the middle of the California desert arose a giant pyramid of light, a modern mystic pagan temple filled with tens of thousands of revelers. Maybe it was the nice weather. Maybe it was the idyllic palm tree-lined setting. Maybe it was the anticipation. But something profound happened beneath that pyramid at the Coachella Valley Music And Arts Festival when The Stooges took the stage.

It was the band's first gig in thirty years. And it was the first time that people who never got to see them the first time around were able to fully understand the band's power, that these guys aren't just the inventors of punk rock. They're philosopher kings. I'd call them shamans, but their douchebag ex-labelmate Jim Morrison has fucked that word up forever and ever as it relates to rock. (Author's note, 2024: In retrospect, a little too harsh, no?)

This reunion show was a long time coming. The ball got rolling earlier this year when The Stooges recorded four new songs for Iggy's upcoming studio album: "Skull Ring," "Little Electric Chair," "Dead Rock Star," and "Loser." Word circulating around the festival was that the band is going to record a new album, and that Jack White is likely to produce it.

But the band didn't play any of those new songs, sticking instead to songs from the first two records. Once the band was on stage, even Iggy had to admit it felt good.

"Are you fucking happy? I think I'm getting fucking happy too! I want to fuck something up!" said the Iguana between songs.

The tribal stomp drums of Scott "Rock Action" Asheton lead the way, and newcomer Minuteman bassist Mike Watt clung on to the low end. Ron Asheton's razor wire guitar solos and chunky power chords provided passion and punctuation.

As for Iggy, as usual, he was jumping and twirling and spitting at the audience. He was gonna make damn sure that everybody knew what was going on.

"Fuckers! Fucking motherfuckers! We are The Stooges!" said Iggy, beginning the band introductions. "I'm fucking Iggy!" It's not as though there was any doubt that he was the man, born James Osterberg, who is known to the world as Iggy Pop. It was said more in a "Song Of Myself" sort of way—you *will* notice me, and you *will* pay attention.

After "T.V. Eye," Iggy talked about how all television shows us is people who are smug and rich and good-looking—people who have it easy. "It makes me feel like fucking dirt!" he said, cueing the band to start "Dirt," a song about feeling and cutting that describes modern separation and solipsism so well that it feels like it could have been written today instead of in 1970.

Near the end of the hour-long set, The Stooges were joined by Steve Mackay blowing free jazz tenor sax as they launched into "1970." The sax

drove the band into frenzy, creating a wailing cacophony of celebration and self-abandonment that would make John Coltrane and Nusrat Fateh Ali Khan smile down from Heaven.

But it was during the climactic "Fun House" that the band really began to travel the spaceways. Iggy sang: "Let me in." Over and over he sang it: "Let me in." Was it some sort of James Brown-esque command to the band?

Something along the lines of "Can we take it to the bridge?" Or was it something more? Maybe it really was the latter. Later on, Iggy sang: "We're feeling separated." Finally, at the end of the song, he sang: "I am you." He repeated: "I am you. I am you."

So if Iggy is us, and we're feeling separated, doesn't it make sense that we should let him in? C'mon in, Iggy; bring the brothers and Watt and Steve, too.

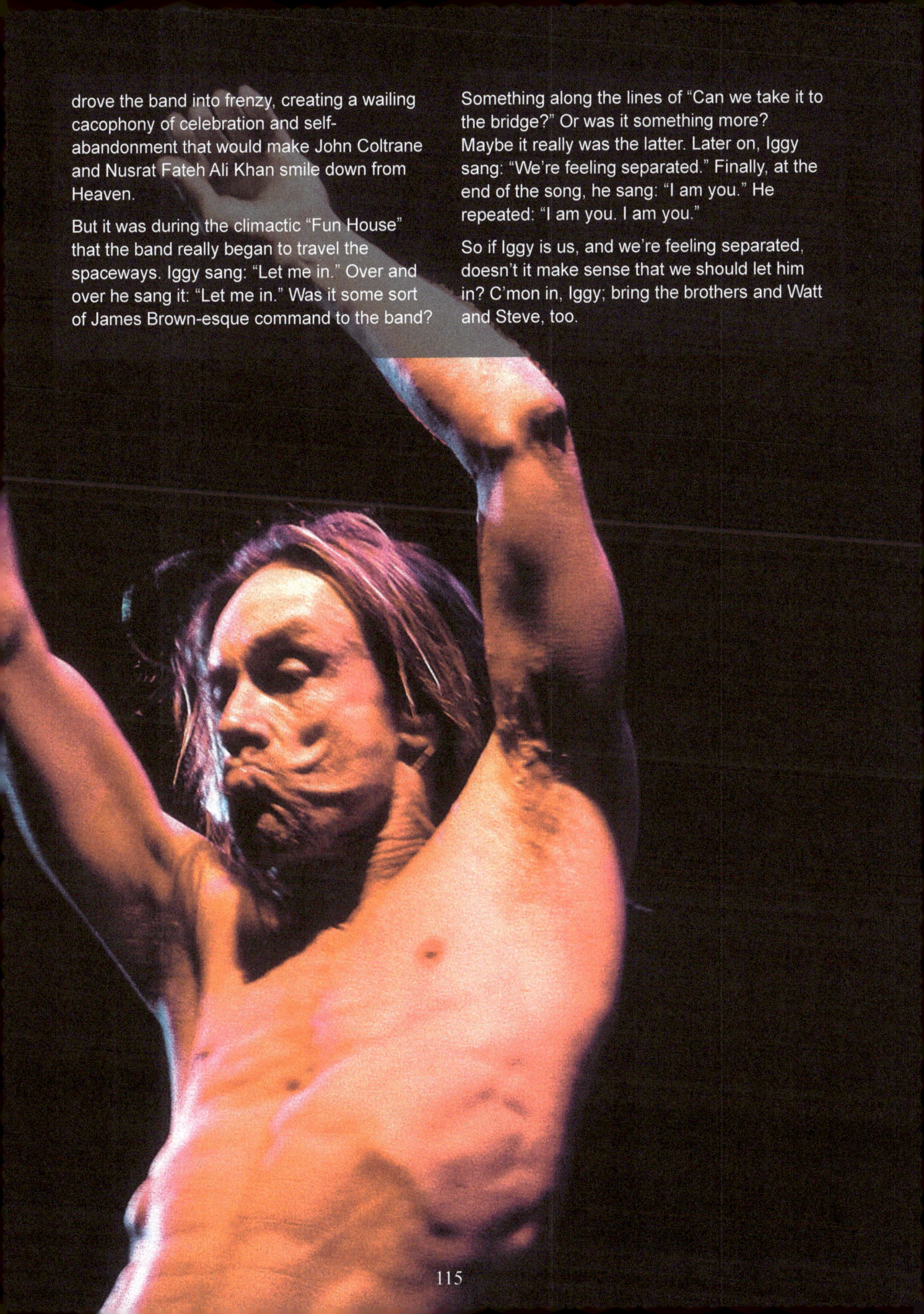

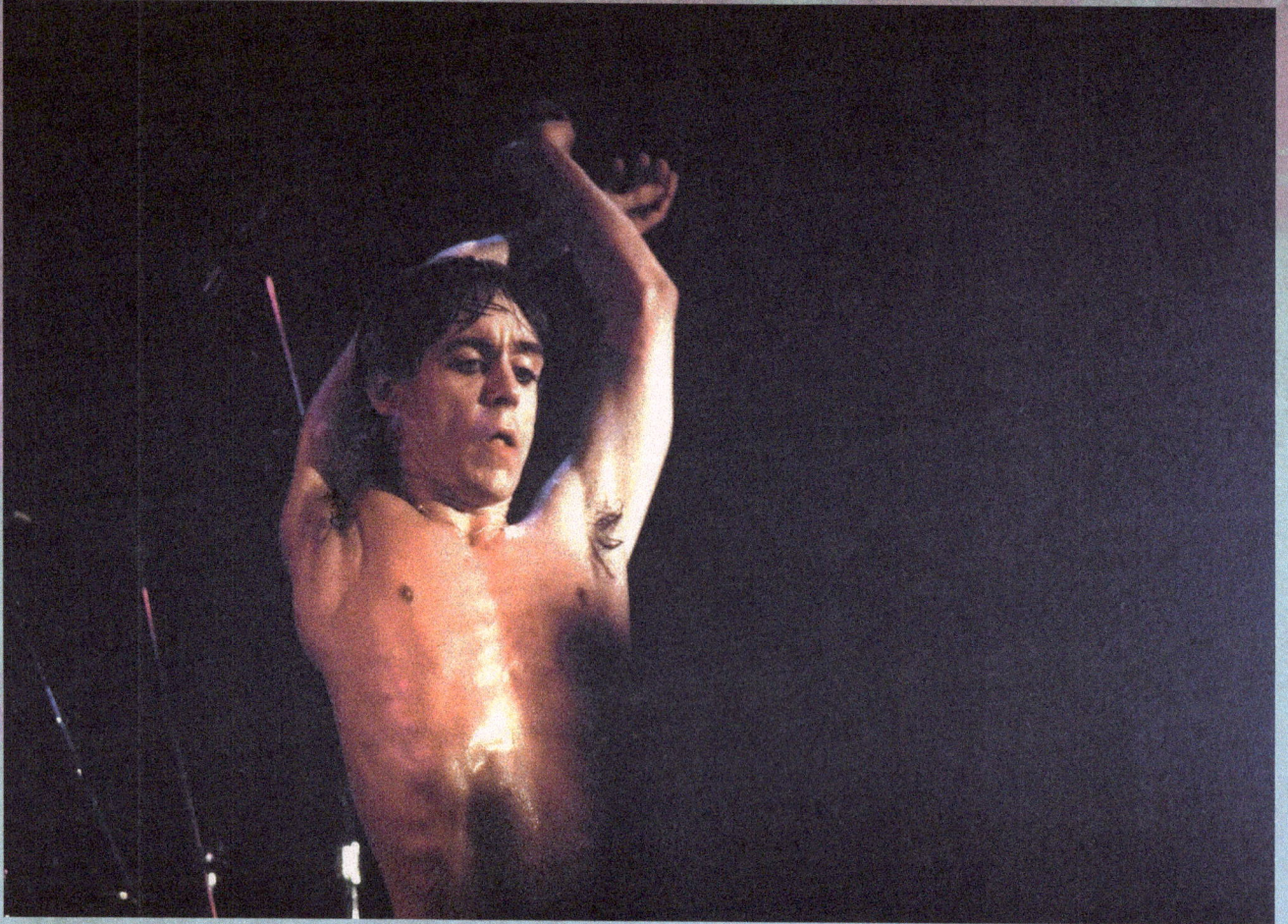

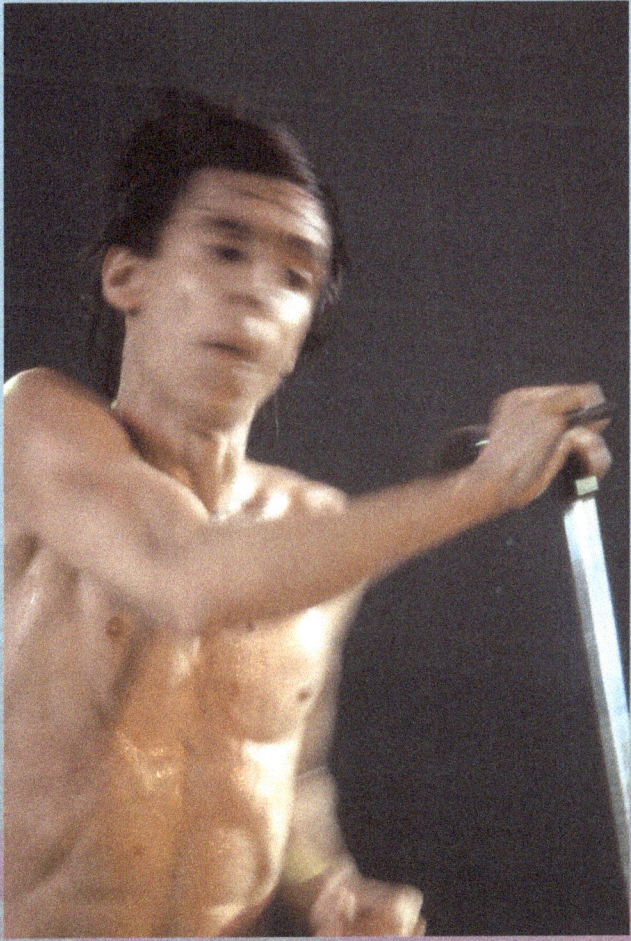
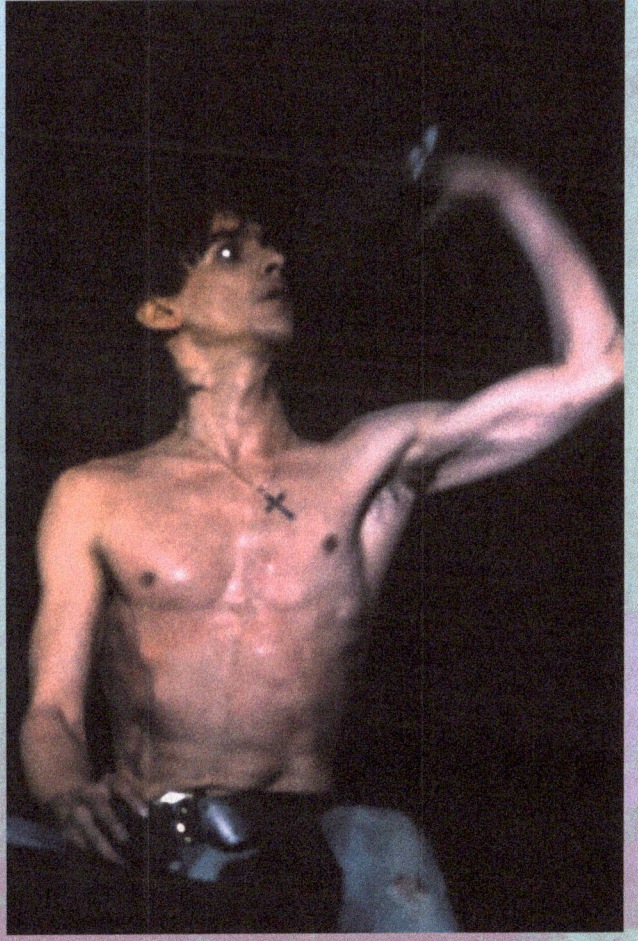

JUDGEMENT AT OSTERBERG

WITHIN THE FIRST WEEK

IGGY POP: Hey Jeffrey, it's Iggy. I gave ya a wild shot and called ya. Missed ya. No problem. Um . . . I'll . . . I'll make it up to you some time in the next . . . Feels like within the next week. All right, later.

WITHIN THE NEXT WEEK

JEFFREY MORGAN: Hello?

IGGY: Hey, is that Jeffrey?

JEFFREY: Yes, this is.

IGGY: Hey, hello.

JEFFREY: How are you doing, sir?

IGGY: Hey, fine. Um . . . Jeffrey, wouldja do me a favor? I'd like to give you a number and ask you to call me back in about five minutes.

JEFFREY: I can't do that 'cause I don't have long distance and I'm just a poor old rock critic.

IGGY: [laughs] All right, well then, uh, let's go ahead then—

JEFFREY: No, no, you—

IGGY: I'll call you back in five minutes.

JEFFREY: You call me back whenever it's good for you, sir.

IGGY: All right, talk to you later.

FIVE MINUTES LATER

JEFFREY: Hello.

IGGY: Hey, Jeffrey.

JEFFREY: Thank you for calling back. I appreciate that.

IGGY: *Sure, sure*. We uh . . . We're going to have to do it and talk in a couple of bits today but, uh, I'm good for a while. I'm uh . . . I'm going . . . I'm in the car on my way to buy some *palm trees*, so I'm—

JEFFREY: Well, I certainly don't want to get in the way of your *gardening* there.

IGGY: [*laughing*] Yeah, exactly right, you know! So, uh . . .

JEFFREY: Every time I talk to Robert, he's talkin' about his *orange trees* in the back yard—

IGGY: *Oh.*

JEFFREY: —so I understand that. But first off, I wanted to thank you for calling—

IGGY: Oh, you betcha.

JEFFREY: The second thing I wanted to say is to offer my sincere condolences on the loss of your friend.

IGGY: Aw, *yeah* . . .

JEFFREY: I mean that sincerely.

IGGY: That's very nice of you. I appreciate it.

JEFFREY: As you know, Robert and I are working on this authorized biography together—

IGGY: I *know* that, I *know* that and, um, this is *great* and if you just wanted to talk, to say hello, or anything, that's great. I was expecting to be, uh—

JEFFREY: Grilled?

IGGY: —*interviewed* in some way, but uh . . .

JEFFREY: No, you're going to be grilled, I'm afraid. I've got a lot of questions about *Raw Power* because it looks like I'm going to be writing the liner notes for the *Raw Power* box set as well.

IGGY: Oh, now you're making my day!

JEFFREY: So I think I might be doing that.

IGGY: All right, well, why don't you go ahead and *shoot* at me and I'll tell ya what I know.

JEFFREY: Now I know that you probably don't *remember* any of this, and if you *don't*, it's okay if you make stuff up and *lie*, because that's okay too.

IGGY: All right.

JEFFREY: But I *do* have to ask you about you and David and whoever else mixed that original *Raw Power* album—and remember, you can take the Fifth any time you want.

IGGY: Go ahead, what specifically?

JEFFREY: Do you know what the recording budget was for that record?

IGGY: Oh, well the sessions, Da— David was *never* present, not even . . . The recording sessions were an engineer—I don't remember his name—an assistant, and, uh, The Stooges. Period. Myself being counted as one of them.

JEFFREY: So you basically ran the session yourself.

IGGY: If there was *ever* a visitor, we weren't thrilled, *that's* for sure, but I don't think we had . . . We had someone to help with the equipment at that time, and I don't remember who. I don't even think Mick Rock came to those . . . Mick Rock photographed us quite a bit in our *rehearsal* room but . . .

David got involved after I'd *ruined* maybe the fifth take of the mix. [*laughing*] Honestly, I became . . . In the words of the guys who are gonna track down and kill Colonel Kurtz in *Apocalypse Now*, after the record I became *unsound*. And no matter *how* I mixed it, it didn't seem to sound . . . The treble couldn't be *trebley* enough, the volume couldn't be *loud* enough, I couldn't be satisfied and I lost my *perspective*.

JEFFREY: Now I *know*, because I've listened exhaustively to that *Fun House* box set—

IGGY: Yeah.

JEFFREY: —and I'm gonna give you what you deserve. You're a professional and you know what you wanted when you were doing that stuff.

IGGY: Yeah.

JEFFREY: Now it's funny because there are *so* many thorough takes all the way through of *Fun House* and there's *so* much professionalism there, but there's *nothing* that exists so far of the *Raw Power* sessions except, basically, what's already been heard. Did you guys run through those numbers repeatedly, take after take, like you did during the *Fun House* sessions?

IGGY: Let me . . . I, you know, I remixed . . . Well, let me back up anyway just to finally clear this up. David Bowie came in for the remix, and that was done in Hollywood, as is common knowledge at, I wanna say Western Recorders. And he used, to his credit, he's a guy who loves being up to the minute, and there was something called a "Time Cube" that had just come out on the gadget market, studio gadget market, and it looked like a bong [*laughs*] that you could attach to a speaker, and you'd play something through it and it made a particular sort of echo and he used it on a couple of Scott's drum tracks and on the guitar on "Gimme Danger." So that is where he came and left on that, was in the mix.

JEFFREY: Yeah, but everything that seems to exist are different variations of mixes of *the same take*. It seems—

IGGY: There's a lot of different mixes on *Raw Power* because I tried mixing it a couple, three times, and as I toldja, I wanted it to sound a certain way and I actually had *gotten* there and then some but I didn't realize it at the time. I lost all perspective.

And what I had going for me on *Fun House*, that I didn't have on *Raw Power*, was that the engineer was *astonishing*. He was *really* good. Brian Ross-Myring. He was an old Englishman who was a yachtsman, public school educated, sort of looked like . . . Like, he could've been an MI6 from . . . He could've been James Bond retired. Silver-haired gent. He had recorded Barbra Streisand. And he happened to know what to *do* with us.

But getting back to *Raw Power*, when I did the remix, you know, I'd heard everything from Bowie saying:

"There were only three tracks, *what could I do?*" to the engineers saying: "They put everything on one . . . we didn't even *use* tracks!" Actually, it was a sixteen track record done on thirteen tracks.

JEFFREY: So you have thirteen tracks, with everything split *onto* thirteen tracks.

IGGY: Yes, exactly. There are thirteen clean tracks on *Raw Power*. And we *did* actually do at least *one* extra song, sorta like *Fun House*. *Fun House* had one or two. *Fun House* had "Lost In The Future" and I think one other. We had one on *Raw Power* and it's . . . [*laughing*] . . . it's *so* not . . . *not* worthy of the record that I *still* can't—even though I just heard it a couple of years ago—I still can't remember the name of it. But, uh, it was our outtake. There was one that *really* just wasn't quite up to it and we didn't put that out.

JEFFREY: On *Fun House*, you did thirty different complete takes of "Loose."

IGGY: Yeah.

JEFFREY: On *Raw Power*, were there ever thirty takes or twenty takes or five or six takes—

IGGY: I would say, if memory serves me, I'd say six to twelve; a little more standard at that point. And that would probably be—now this is *my* version—because for *Raw Power* we were much better rehearsed. In other words, nobody was gonna make a mistake. [*laughing*] And the songs were a little more written out whereas on *Fun House* I was still . . . *creating* some of the lyrics at the last minute—and in *my* memory, *Dave* was prone to make a mistake although, you know what? *I heard it back*. And being The Stooges, we didn't do what, you know . . . if there was a mistake, we started over. We didn't just drop it in or edit it or anything . . . [*laughing*] . . . we're not like that.

But now Ron tells me . . . or I think it was, um, the so-called producer, the babysitter on *Fun House*, that told me, no, no it was *my* idea to get you guys to do a lot of takes to have a chance to figure out how to fend for your songs, you know?

What I remember is, basically, in *Fun House*, it was . . one day would be the day of . . . this is the day of "Song X" . . . this is the day of "Loose" . . . this is the day of "Down On The Street" . . . and we're gonna play it 'til we think it's great. And somehow we ended up doin' a lot of takes. And, um, I think . . . I remember myself being critical . . . *details* would matter to me in the jamming that might not matter . . . that somebody else might not notice. Because the songs on *Fun House* were so very basic, to hold *up* as songs, they had to be played flawlessly, I felt. They had to be played with a certain commitment—and that wasn't there on every take, you know.

JEFFREY: So there *are* other takes that should be there somewhere in the vault, that weren't used.

IGGY: Yeah, they're good and there are quite a few takes on *Raw Power* but not as many as *Fun House* for some reason.

JEFFREY: Well, it's good to know that they *exist*.

IGGY: Yeah, they're there.

JEFFREY: And when you did that first mix, who *rejected* that? Was that Defries, or was that Columbia? Who said: "No, this has to be redone."

IGGY: The whole project, again, as *I* remember . . . if it was Columbia, then it was Defries who told me. But I would say Defries. I was *nev*— I had *no* contact at anytime with anyone from the record company, ever. We were signed to MainMan, in effect, and they did . . it was kinda the situation with, like, TLC and Pebbles, you know? [*laughing*] Basically, the classic production contract exploitation situation.

JEFFREY: About your *Raw Power* remix—

IGGY: We didn't have a record contract, we *thought* we did. We were ignorant of the business and, in fact, *he* had a contract with Columbia to deliver the zombie—being *me* and any band I was in—to deliver an album to them x number of times, you know.

JEFFREY: About your *Raw Power* remix—

IGGY: I *did* meet . . . I met Clive Davis *once* and, uh, and, um—

JEFFREY: You tap-danced your way into his heart.

IGGY: Yeah, something like that. Actually, I think he just wanted to get me outta the office. This was one of those classic exec— They picked us up because he passed on David Bowie. That's what *happened*. He passed on David Bowie, realized his *error*, and what an exec does *then* . . . it makes him very liable to pick up *another* act by the same manager or sometimes from the same town. If you passed on Aerosmith, then you pick up J. Geils so you can say you were *involved* in the general movement.

JEFFREY: That's how Decca ended up with the Rolling Stones; because they passed on The Beatles.

IGGY: There you go.

JEFFREY: I mean, it's a tradition that goes back to the start of electricity.

IGGY: Yeah. So that's how *that* happened. And the only other person I met, who was a real gent, although it was pretty funny, at the *very* butt end of our time there when they actually *did* release *Raw Power* . . . Goddard Lieberson, who was the grey eminence . . . he was, like, a Columbia CEO—

JEFFREY: Oh yeah, he's a legend.

IGGY: Yeah, he's a legend. He had a beautiful suit on, he looked like Leonard Bernstein. And we had our party decorated with, um, those little . . . You know those little plastic fake *vomits* that people used to put on the floor? [*laughter*] And he had to pick his way through the plastic vomits to come to our record release party. Robert Plant came, to his credit. He was curious about us, so . . .

JEFFREY: You're such a fun-loving guy, I'm still trying to figure out what nice guy like you is doing in a book like this.

IGGY: [*laughing*] There you go.

JEFFREY: Listen, about your *Raw Power* remix . . .

IGGY: Yeah.

JEFFREY: When you sang: "Look out honey, I'm using technology," you weren't kidding around, were ya?

IGGY: Well, not at the . . . not at the time, you know? I mean—

JEFFREY: Look, I don't mind that your remix of *Raw Power* is the loudest album in history. As a matter of fact, speaking as a volume advocate from *way* back, I *applaud* you for mixing an album that's *so* loud you don't even have to turn your *amp* on to hear it.

IGGY: [*laughing*]

JEFFREY: And I don't mind that you extended some of the openings and the endings to the songs, but speaking on behalf of everyone who has that album memorized note for note, I *really* have a problem with how you faded down some of James Williamson's original guitar parts and faded up brand new ones, especially on "Your Pretty Face Is Going To Hell."

IGGY: Now—

JEFFREY: Because you listen to that song, and you've got it memorized, and then, all of a sudden, this other car comes around the corner that you have never seen before—and it's kind of disconcerting.

IGGY: [*laughing*] I couldn't agree with you more!

JEFFREY: Then why did you *do* it, sir?

IGGY: Well, I had . . . you know . . . [*laughing*] It *seemed* like a good idea . . .

JEFFREY: As I say in the biography, we all know which road is paved with good intentions.

IGGY: I don't . . . I *had* no good intentions in the remix. The only reason I *did* it was . . . It was entirely *cynical*. American rock . . . The band had never got its *due* in America. American rock at the time was dominated by *jarheads*. And I could see that loud and hyper-manly was a coming thing, uh . . . Hold on a moment.

[*Talking to Nina*] You what? You want that? Just what street? I don't know.

Hey, uh . . .

JEFFREY: You gotta call me back?

IGGY: I'll call you back.

JEFFREY: All right, man.

IGGY: Bye.

[*slight pause whilst he adjusts his accoutrements*]

JEFFREY: Hello again!

IGGY: Hey Jeffrey, if it's okay with you, I'm gonna . . . I wanna answer what you asked me and then maybe talk about another ten minutes and then, if I can, I'd like to call you back late in the afternoon. Will that work for you?

JEFFREY: I don't want to get in the way of the palm trees.

IGGY: Hey, listen, what I was gettin' at with the *Raw Power* was basically, the whole thing, they never promoted it properly, people weren't hearin' it in the U.S., people thought Smashing Pumpkins were heavy, they though that Fred Durst—whatever that band was—they thought *that* was heavy. Rollins had muscles, and it was just . . . The whole thing was pissin' me off [*laughs*] and they came . . . basically they came to me and said: "Look, if *you'll* do a remix, *we'll* do a reissue." So I thought: "Okay, I'll do the remix." And once I was gonna do it, then I kinda did it on steroids.

JEFFREY: Like I said, you were using technology and you weren't kidding.

IGGY: Well, a lot of people *did* complain about the *sound* of the original *Raw*—

JEFFREY: Not anymore!

IGGY: So now they love it.

JEFFREY: After they heard *yours* and had gotten their *ears* surgically repaired? "You don't know what you've got 'till it's gone." People *really* like that original mix now.

IGGY: Well, there ya go. So that's *great*. You know, at least . . . Somebody looked up the SoundScan for me after I did that, and ten times the number of people went out and bought it than bought it before.

JEFFREY: Oh, I know people who bought their first compact disc players when your *Raw Power* remix came out.

IGGY: Yeah, so whatever happens next, who knows? [*laughing*] Maybe I'll let *Williamson* try one, *I* don't know.

JEFFREY: When you—

IGGY: Jeffrey, I'm . . . *We're lost.* Lemme call you back when we find out where we are.

JEFFREY: Okay, good luck!

IGGY: Thank you, buddy.

[*after they find out where they are*]

JEFFREY: Hello *again*.

IGGY: [*laughing*] You know, these things happen!

JEFFREY: Listen, I feel real bad about seriously cutting into your Valentine's Day time, so why don't you just go and enjoy your day, how does that sound?

IGGY: Hey, that's a beautiful thing.

JEFFREY: Have fun and thanks very much.

IGGY: All right, man.

126

JAMES WILLIAMSON

photographed by
Robert Matheu
in Hollywood on August 12th 2009

All the Best Jeffery

jeffery
yr
A
smartASS
watch it ~
Iggy

IT TAKES ONE TO KNOW ONE

In 2009, when Iggy Pop met with James Williamson to discuss the future of Iggy And The Stooges, it was the first time the two had been in the same room together since 1979; thirty long years. And, well-mannered boy that he is, Iggy invited Robert Matheu to join them.

Now by this time two things had happened: First, I had spoken to Iggy on the chatterline, taking him to task for his revisonist *Raw Power* remix. Second, I had paid short shrift to much of Iggy's solo career when I reviewed *The Weirdness* in the authorized Stooges biography. Having read what I'd written, Iggy took umbrage and mentioned it to Robert, who defended me *in absentia* by saying: "Yeah, but he liked *The Weirdness!*"

So when Robert attended the meeting, he brought along two 11 x 14 prints of his most iconic Stooges photo and asked if they'd sign one for himself, which they gladly did. Then Robert presented them with the second print, saying: "This one is for my friend Jeffrey." Whereupon James signed his name at the top first, with Iggy signing his name at the bottom second, just as they had done on the first print. Then, noticing my name at the top in James' personal inscription, Iggy paused.

"Wait a minute," he said, looking over at Robert. "Is this the same guy I spoke to on the telephone?"

"Yeah!" Robert cheerfully confirmed. "That's Jeffrey!"

"Oh!" replied Iggy, tilting his head back with a knowing look of recognition. Whereupon Dr. Sigmund Stooge picked up the silver marker and added a psychological profile over his signature. Then, with a big smile on his face, Iggy handed the print back to Robert saying: "The dude's pretty weird, ha ha ha, but that's okay because I'm weird too!"

Columbia Records commissioned me to write these liner notes for their 2010 Raw Power Deluxe Edition *box set. Unfortunately, they never saw print because the document file containing them was stolen off a shared drive in the art department at Sony Music Entertainment. And because I had lost my own backup copy due to a mysterious DDoS attack, I was unable to supply them with a duplicate. Years later, I received a faded printout of my original notes inside an envelope postmarked Tijuana. Printed in lipstick at the top of the first page was a cryptic lower case message: "gracias por el 'prestamo' xx"*

AMERICAN SEIZURE

"Maybe I was, uh, what you nowadays call a *stooge*, huh?"

— Joseph Cotton in *Citizen Kane*, 1941

SIDE ONE:
RUNNIN' LOW ON A-MEMORY

They came, they saw, they conked out—and then they left.
But just like General Douglas MacArthur, they returned.

"With *Raw Power*, The Stooges return with a vengeance, exhibiting all the ferocity that characterizes them at their livid best. The Igg. Nobody does it better, nobody does it, period. When you're talking about the O mind, the very central eye of the universe that opens up like a huge, gaping, sucking maw, step aside for The Stooges."
— Lenny Kaye, *Rolling Stone*

"The band accelerates beyond anything that's been recorded, or played live or even dreamed of, in years. Only a truly diabolical mind could have made the best album of the '70s and Iggy apparently has it because he's summed up everything in eight songs."
— Dave Marsh, CREEM

"The monolith of the age. I would've given all my teeth just to have that beast be a double album."
— Lester Bangs, CREEM

Those three quotes weren't written decades after the dust had settled and cooler heads had prevailed, they were penned with passion and precision in the heat of the moment shortly after *Raw Power*'s initial North American release in February of 1973; indeed, the first two were actually used in Columbia Records' original print ad for the album—and for good reason:

Nobody does it better. The best album of the '70s. Beyond anything that's been recorded in years. Truly diabolical. Return with a vengeance. At their livid best. All the ferocity. Step aside. Nobody does it, period.

Those aren't ordinary statements made lightly because they don't describe an ordinary album meant to be played lightly. More than any other words which have subsequently been written, these initial comments cut to the core and best explain why so many people around the world, both ardent fans and professional musicians alike, *still* consider *Raw Power* to be *the* ultimate manifestation of rock 'n' roll incarnate in its purest and most uninhibited form—an album created by four musicians who were literally possessed with an uncanny preternatural intuitive understanding of what primal rock music really *is*, and Poppiously blessed with the innate ability and supreme confidence to create it at will, *no matter what the personal or professional cost.*

That's not a bad birthright to leave behind, especially since *Raw Power* isn't even a real Stooges album to begin with. For one thing, if you want to get technical about it, unlike their pioneering prototypical debut album and idiot savant garde jazzbo follow-up, *Raw Power* has never been officially credited solely to "The Stooges." In fact, a number of first edition copies of *Raw Power* proclaimed just the opposite by excising the band completely with a front cover accreditation that simply shrieked "IGGY" in large dripping letters aptly appropriated from *The Munsters* via the original oozing logo of the world's most notorious horror comic, EC's *Tales From The Crypt*—which makes perfect sense in light of Iggy's opening invocation on the album's title track.

Less apparent, however, is the hidden rationale behind that brief title tag, which was a begrudging die-hard holdover from the early days when the record that would become *Raw Power* was originally slated to be the first Iggy Pop *solo* album instead. That The Stooges even played on it at all was more out of dire necessity than anything else given that it was *The Igg* who was originally signed to MainMan by Tony Defries, *not* The Stooges.

Of far greater importance, however, is the absolutely crucial fact that *Raw Power* doesn't feature Ron Asheton on guitar—and it's an invariable axiom that a "Stooges" album without Ron's signature wah-wah on it just isn't a *Stooges* album, son.

So if you fervently regard *Fun House* to be the best Stooges album ever, the good news is that, technically, you can continue to keep that belief,

safe in the knowledge that you can also accord *Raw Power* the same maximum respect that any estranged and slightly deranged distant relative demands. And make no mistake, this is a *very* demanding album.

The even *better* news is that *Raw Power* has more than enough spilled family blood surging through its engorged veins to ensure that this black sheep is one horse-dicked freak of a beast that will *never* wind up in anybody's bathroom overdosed and on its knees. If you think you can live with *that*, then maybe you'll have what it takes to carefully approach this aberrant patchwork Frankenstooge creation and ultimately accept it on the only terms that it'll ever accept *you* on: its own. Quite a good scene, isn't it? One band crazy, four very sane creators.

Understandably, ethnomusicologists thought otherwise. After all, anyone who's inclined to sit around with a buncha high falutin elitist academic eggheads and have intimate little tête-à-têtes about the arcane minutiae of some obscure backwater record label no one's ever heard of is *way* too hoity-toity to heft the harsh-hewn cudgel that is *Raw Power.*

Which isn't to say that blue-collar critics were any savvier when it came to sussing out the situation. Even the most astute Igg adherents, many of whom thought they knew the full extent of what The Stooges were capable of, never received the slightest advance warning that something hazardous was lethally hurtling towards them at breakneck speed until it was too late and the rumbling Motor City muscle machine had already smearcased them under its mag wheels.

They never knew what hit them because, boosted by the Asheton's tightly coiled Double Rocker heavy-hemi engine and sparked by Williamson's high combustion guitar, crazy driver Iggy had upped the ante and exceeded all expectations by revving the fresh-off-the-blocks souped up Stoogemobile into overdrive and laying down a smoldering patch that left everyone blindsided and choking on their spume. But as every Kustom Kulture King from Ed "Big Daddy" Roth to George Barris knows, the transformation from junkyard heap to supercharged muscle car can often be an arduous one—and nothing was more difficult to deal with than the delicate matter of Ron's hypothetical "demotion" from guitar to bass.

Yet whenever the subject was broached in the past, James Williamson, to his everlasting credit, always steadfastly maintained that his decision to enlist the once and future Stooges guitarist to play bass on *Raw Power* was the right one. That he still does today isn't a belated attempt at retrospective fence-mending on James' part, it's the learned opinion of a man who first played guitar alongside a bass playing Ron Asheton when they were both in high school and members of the Chosen Few.

(Note from James Williamson: "I never played in the Chosen Few at the same time as Ron Asheton, I preceded him.")

Furthermore, as both the *Raw Power* album itself and surviving subsequent live tour tapes ably attest, Ron truly was an exceptionally dexterous bassist who was equally adept at slamming four stings as he was at shredding six.

Another reason why nobody ever indignantly objected to Ron Asheton playing bass on *Raw Power* is because his understudy turned out to be the Roy Hobbs of rock 'n' roll. James Williamson was a heretofore unknown "natural" who seemingly came out of nowhere, stepped up to the plate, and then proceeded to repeatedly crush them out of the park in spectacular fashion before vanishing back into the ether. It's not that James was in any way a *better* guitarist than Ron, it's just that his entire approach to the instrument was so radically *different* from how Ron played—and from what The Stooges had previously been used to—that any possible comparison of the two was pointless.

There's also no denying the unassailable fact that it's James' unreasonable sledgehammer guitar which accounts in large part for the record's enormous enduring and endearing influence. *Raw Power*—was there ever an album more aptly named—would never have been able to live up to its title without his singular swath-cutting style which simultaneously pierced *and* pummeled. It's an astonishing accomplishment made all the more extraordinary since the only other guitarists on the planet at that time who came even *remotely* close to matching James toe to toe for such sheer unhinged and unbridled ferocity were Jeff Beck and Mick Ronson in England—and even *they* seemed like a couple of dainty doilies next to the buffeting slabs of sound that the Strait James Insurgency was relentlessly cranking out. Meanwhile, back in the States, his

audacious axe work was deemed so radically raucous that, by default, The Skull was universally ranked number one in a field of one.

SIDE TWO: GOIN' DOWN IN A-HISTORY

Although a surfeit of slapdash bootlegs abounded, ardent Stoogeologists were baffled for decades over the dire dearth of high quality *Raw Power* outtakes. It wasn't until the very end of the last century, however, that it looked like their long-playing prayers would finally be answered. If Iggy's 1997 audio exhumation that turned up the music Hi as Fi can go only added more fuel to their desire to hear additional master tapes, then it was the 1999 release of the revelatory limited edition box set *1970: The Complete Fun House Sessions* that fully inflamed their studio starved salivations. For after hearing those seven discs which definitively delineated The Stooges' recording methodology over a period of eight sequential hours, who could be blamed for wishfully thinking that it surely would only be a matter of time before Columbia likewise saw the light and released *1972: The Complete Raw Power Sessions*.

But the painstaking decade-long search for *Raw Power* outtakes is nothing compared to the painful decades-long debate that continued to rage over the record's final mix—a hellacious hullabaloo which has necessitated nothing less than the creation of this very box set over 35 years after the fact. And although *nobody* who bought the album in 1973 liked what they heard, such is *Raw Power*'s inexorably bludgeoning force that even the original universally reviled "all Jim and James, no Ronnie or Scottie" mix was unable to wound the album, let alone kill it—not that some didn't have murder in their eyes from the first moment that they heard the final vinyl's sonic reduction, none more so than an irate Rock Action who pitched the platter out his front door after listening to it.

However, at the risk of this underhanded overview becoming *Dr. Stoogelove or: How I Learned To Stop Worshipping And Drop The Pop*, it behooves me to point out that there are a number of real good reasons as to why the 1973 version now solidly sits supreme in the hearts and mind rooms of listeners worldwide; not the least of which is The Igg's very own remix/remauling which provided a much needed frame of reference against which the original offering could be retroactively reassessed, frequently with favorable results. I could go on, so I will.

One could easily argue that a key component of *Raw Power*'s perverse appeal lies in the way that it subliminally seduces you into thinking that all eight of its album tracks were recorded and mixed by eight different entities with equally divergent sensibilities. You'd need an advanced Masters degree in forensic music to find any remnants of the tactical air strikes, sword fights, and backing vocals which are said to be buried somewhere deep within the confines of its enveloping quicklime sound. Yet despite this unified disparity, most of what *can* be heard, with very few exceptions, incongruously appears in back to mono mode, save for the ominous anomalous stereo echo effect or cross-channel pan which is abruptly dropped in. The resulting sudden shock effect is easily the aural equivalent of William Castle unexpectedly inserting thick gouts of bright red blood into his black and white psychotronic film *The Tingler*. And you're still wondering why there's monster movie lettering on the front cover . . .

But every house of horrors has its share of charnel casualties and *Raw Power* is no exception to the ghoul. Not always, but certainly more often than not, Ron Asheton's bass playing is criminally certified MIA, never to be found. And if the drummer *does* manage to have a slightly higher survival rate, it's only because Scott Asheton repeatedly makes a valiant powerhouse attempt to rise up out of the swirling vortex only to be pulled back under. Meanwhile, the singer and the guitarist are slugging it out in a brutal bare-knuckled brawl for sonic supremacy that will ultimately end with their entire world crashing down around them, leaving everyone buried alive in the ooze.

Yet not only did the album survive, it continues to thrive. Of course it does. How could it not when, in a singular cataclysm of convergence, the Fates aligned to ensure that its lyrics would be so minimally insightful and its musicianship so muscularly inciteful? And how else to explain what happened on the evening of September 31st 1972 when a studio engineer inadvertently bulk erased the *Raw Power* master tapes, only to find every track inexplicably intact the very next morning—as if the music had somehow reconstituted itself overnight.

My friend, can you prove that it *didn't* happen?

And do you *feel* that beat?

There have been a lot of proclamations about the ground zero of punk rock, but for me, it is Iggy And The Stooges' *Raw Power* album. The Stooges sounded like no one else when they crawled out of the sludge of the Detroit suburbs in 1969. They were already rebels without a cause, channeling every bit of teenage disdain for the older generation combined with the swagger of hyper-charged sexual creatures on the prowl.

The primal grooves and distortion were already there on *The Stooges* and its 1970 follow-up *Fun House*, but the fully formed manifesto of punk arrived with *Raw Power*. The addition of James Williamson on lead guitar took the sound from a smoldering groove to a blast of abrasive howl that terrifies and thrills in equal measure. Iggy's lyrics are more ferocious as well. Just listen to the lyrics of the album opener, "Search And Destroy" . . .

I'm a street-walkin' cheetah with a heart full of napalm.
I'm a runaway son of the nuclear A-bomb.
I am the world's forgotten boy.
The one who searches and destroys.

Iggy created punk's *raison d'être* in four lines. However, The Stooges were not one-dimensional, and *Raw Power* offered more than proto-punk. Songs like "Gimme Danger" and "I Need Somebody" slow down the tempo and blend Velvet Underground garage with the crooning of a deranged Jim Morrison, plus a dash of psychedelia. The album has a nod to glam rock but with a lot more dirt than glamour. *Raw Power* blew people's minds when it came out, and it still sounds urgent, vital, and threatening to this day.

Lots of folks have tried, but *Raw Power* can't be beat!

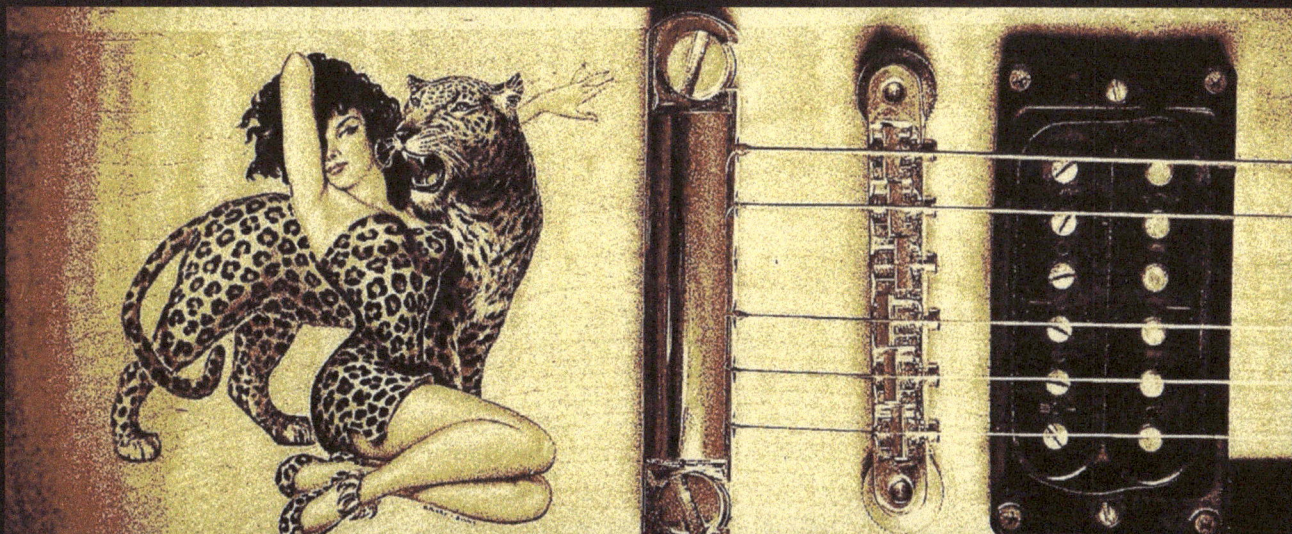

JESUS LOVES THE STOOGES

Of course He does. How could He not when there is no partiality with God? That's why Jesus loves The Stooges' fans as well. Yes, even you. Especially you. And I love that He's given me this opportunity to thank Him first and foremost for making this book possible— but He's not the only one to whom I have to say well, well, ladies and gentlemen, thank you for your kind indulgence.

● I'm eternally and deeply indebted to my parents, **Anne Morgan** and **Joe Morgan**, for a lifetime of unconditional love and lenience—especially when I was in playing loud rock 'n' roll music all day and out photographing loud rock 'n' roll concerts all night.

● Words cannot express my heartfelt gratitude to **Teddie Dahlin**, the visionary CEO of New Haven Publishing, without whom there would be no Stooges book for you to read. Having already published *Rock Critic Confidential* and *Alice Cooper Confidential*, she wanted *Iggy And The*

Stooges: The Authorized Biography to be the capstone of my Rock Critic Trilogy. And speaking of trifectas . . .

● This is the third time that **Pete Cunliffe** has designed a book of mine, with each successive volume looking better than the previous one. That's because Pete *gets it*, which makes my job a breeze, knowing that the finished product is going to be a stone gas. So if you dig what you see, credit Pete because the cat always makes me look good.

● I literally can't thank **Sheryl Matheu** enough for her enduring friendship and for graciously allowing me to extensively use the words and photographs of her late husband, *photographer extraordinaire* Robert Matheu. And although his images are also on ample display in my first two books, I know that my good friend Robert would be especially pleased to see "our book" back in print to entertain a whole new generation of readers.

● A tip of the Boy Howdy! hat to my three

esteemed CREEM colleagues **Dave DiMartino**, **Ivan Suvanjieff**, and **Brian J. Bowe** for agreeing to have their writing reprinted in this new expanded edition.

• I'm indebted to my good friend **John Catto** for contributing the photographs he took of Iggy And The Stooges at the Victory Burlesque in 1974. Although I didn't meet John until 1977 when he was lead guitarist for The Diodes, I subsequently learned that we had both attended many of the same concerts prior to that, The Stooges being one of them.

• Likewise, I'm sure, to fellow shutterbugs **Robert Sikora**, **Jeff Magnum**, **Ralph Alfonso**, **Carlos Llano**, and **Frankie N. Carranza**.

• Mere words cannot convey my profound appreciation for the encouragement and support shown to me over the decades by **Toby Mamis**, **Alice Cooper**, **James Williamson**, and **Iggy Pop**.

• **Eileen Dunsmuir**, you know how grateful I am for your love and godly advice!

• A penultimate word of thanks to activist and artist **Shepard Fairey** for writing the Afterword. As recounted earlier, all I wanted was permission to reprint a few of his previously published words, but Shepard insisted on taking time out of his busy globetrotting schedule to exclusively write something brand new for you to read.

• Finally, a very special thank you to **James Williamson** for writing the Introduction to this book. "I'd be honored," was his gracious reply when I asked him if he'd care to write a few words, but the honor is all mine because I've remained a big fan of Strait James' uncanny influential guitar playing ever since I bought my first copy of *Raw Power* at Sam The Record Man back in February of 1973.

• Oh, and lest I forget: As always, my sincere and utmost thanks to *you* for your support; may God bless!

Rock 'n' Roll's Most Entertaining Writer

JEFFREY MORGAN

ROCK CRITIC CONFIDENTIAL
by JEFFREY MORGAN

Authorized biographer of
ALICE COOPER *and* IGGY POP & THE STOOGES

ROCK 'N' ROLL'S MOST ENTERTAINING WRITER
FIFTY YEARS OF WIT AND WISDOM

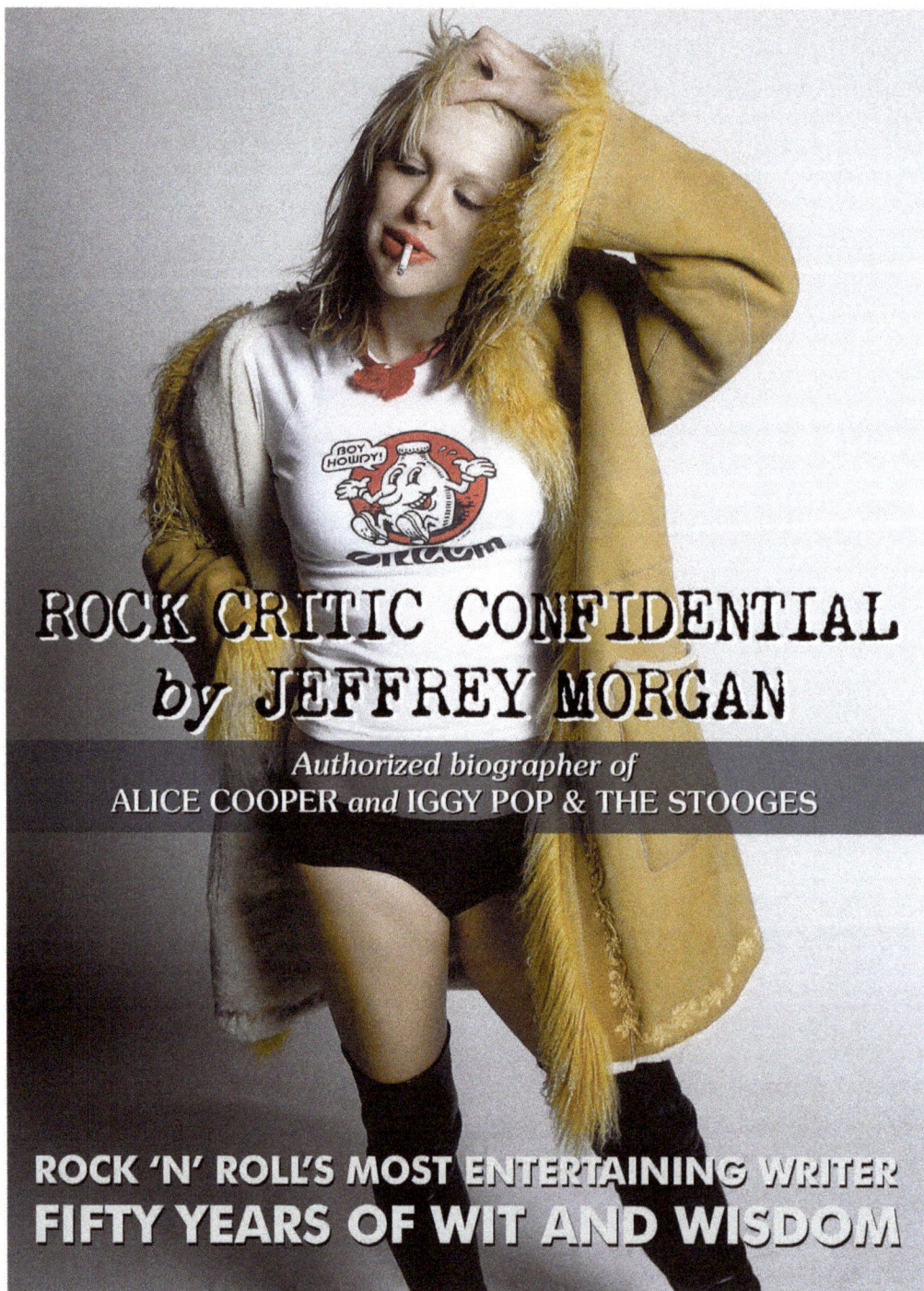

Afterword by Alice Cooper
ON SALE EVERYWHERE

Brought to you from your friends at New Haven Publishing

Rock 'n' Roll's Most Entertaining Writer
JEFFREY MORGAN

"Ladies and gentlemen,
it pleased me very much this evening

to introduce to you a most *powerful* band,

The Stooges!"

www.ingramcontent.com/pod-product-compliance
Lightning Source LLC
Chambersburg PA
CBHW062008150426
42812CB00013BA/2578

* 9 7 8 1 9 1 5 9 7 5 0 4 1 *